Wavelength

Elementary • Coursebook

Kathy
Burke

Julia
Brooks

Longman

Contents

Skills

Skills
Listening: getting to know people
Listening: talking about people
Listening: checking in at reception Writing and speaking: filling in forms
Listening: time and numbers

Wavelength pages

Reading: people at work Listening and speaking: a job interview Writing and speaking: work and play	*Skills* **Reading, listening, speaking** The Oasis Leisure Centre
Reading: a letter home Speaking: *Do you ever . . . ? How often do you . . . ?*	*Conversations* **Help!** Phoning a hotel Understanding signs Pron: intonation
Listening: likes and dislikes; *The Real You!* questionnaire; working with *Mr Perfect* Speaking: *What can you do?*	*Day to day English* **Offers** Looking after guests Saying *Yes* and *No* to offers Pron: weak forms
Speaking: *Are you a "phonaholic"?* questionnaire; *My wonderful life!* Listening: phone conversations Reading: a letter to a friend	*Do you remember?* **Units 1–4** 1 *What's the question?* 2 Lifestyles and leisure 3 *Usually* or *now?* 4 *What do you say?*
Listening: clothes; in a shop Writing and speaking: clothes and fashion Reading: The Fashion Maze	*Day to day English* **Permission** *Can I . . . ?* Vocabulary: things in a living room; collocation of nouns and verbs
Listening: a TV news programme; a radio news interview Reading: a newspaper article Speaking: *When did you last . . . ?* questionnaire	*Conversations* **Oh, really?** Keeping conversations going Intonation ↗ or ↘

Skills	Wavelength pages
Reading: a letter to a friend Listening: Liz's holiday; disagreement Speaking: *Do you like travelling?; Where did you go?*	*Skills* **Reading, speaking** Murder at Hadley Hall!
Speaking: a travel questionnaire; *Excuses, excuses* Reading and listening: a cartoon story Listening: apologising for being late	*Do you remember?* **Units 5–8** 1 Talking about places 2 *Where were you?* 3 *He looks fantastic!* 4 The hotel receptionist game
Reading and listening: a filmscript Listening: a Hollywood agent phones the stars Speaking: making a film	*Conversations* **Oh, no!** Reactions: *That sounds nice; You're joking!* Telling a story
Speaking: *Are you organised?* questionnaire; *Are you busy?* Listening: plans for the weekend Reading and writing: e-mails about arrangements	*Day to day English* **Arrangements** Saying *Yes* and *No* to invitations Making suggestions
Listening and speaking: talking about lunch; a horrible restaurant Speaking: *What food and drink do you like?*	*Skills* **Listening, reading, writing** The Great British breakfast?
Listening: hotels; asking about places; radio ads Speaking: comparing places Writing and speaking: designing products and ads	*Do you remember?* **Units 9–12** 1 Classroom madness! 2 Shopping trolleys 3 *When are they doing that?* 4 Comparing places
Listening: fears Reading: magazine article about fear Speaking: *Have you ever . . . ?*	*Day to day English* **Intonation** Ordering a meal in a restaurant Listening and Pron: polite and rude intonation
Listening and speaking: describing views; music for places Reading, speaking and listening: *My favourite place* Writing and speaking: the perfect place	*Skills* **Reading, writing** Visit the East End!
Listening: illnesses; Charlie's terrible week Reading and speaking: *Do you look after yourself?* questionnaire; Paradise Hall health farm brochure Writing: a diary for Paradise Hall	*Conversations* **Oh, I know . . .** Keeping conversations going; showing interest and reacting
Listening and speaking: daydreaming about the future Writing and speaking: future plans Speaking: *What do you want to do? What are you going to do?*	*Do you remember?* **Units 13–16** 1 Find the mistakes 2 *What's the matter with him / her?* 3 *Who's going to jump out of the balloon?*

By the sea

Present Simple of *be*: *I, you, we, they*
Countries, nationalities and languages
Pronunciation: phonemics, word stress,
    sentence stress

Present Simple of *be*: *I, you, we, they*

1 **a)** Look at the photograph.
Read the sentences (a–h) and
match them to these answers.

Example: a) = 1 Yes I am.

2 ☐ Poland.
3 ☐ Hi, I'm Anna. Nice to meet
    you.
4 ☐ Felix.
5 ☐ Tokyo.
6 ☐ No, we aren't. We're from
    Italy.
7 ☐ Yes, they are.
8 ☐ No, I'm here on business.

b) 🔊 1 Listen and check.

2 **a)** Fill in the gaps.

Example: A: Where are you
                from?
            B: I'm from Sydney.

1 A: .... you from Spain?
  B: No, we .... We..........
    from Argentina.
2 A: .... you Tom?
  B: Yes, I ....
3 A: .... they English or
    American?
  B: They.......... English.
4 A: Where .... your
    children?
  B: They.......... in the shop.
5 A: .... you Portuguese?
  B: No, I.......... . I..........
    Brazilian.

b) 🔊 2 Listen and check.

Are you
Australian?

Hello,
I'm Tom.

Are you here
on holiday?

Are they yo
children?

e
Where are you from?
f
Are you from Spain?
g
What part of Japan are you from?
h
What's your name?

Countries, nationalities and languages

3 **a)** In pairs. Fill in the nationalities and languages.

Country	Nationality	Language
1 Italy	Italian	
2 Argentina		
3 Brazil		
4 Spain		
5 Poland		
6 Germany		
7 The USA		
8 Japan		
9 Portugal		

b) Look at the Word list on page 129 and check.

Pronunciation

Phonemics

4 These words are in phonemic script. How do we write them? Look at the Guide to pronunciation on page 143 for help. Then practise saying the words.

Example: /ˈwelkəm/ = welcome

1 /ˈweɪvleŋθ/ 2 /ˈlæŋgwɪdʒ/ 3 /ˈbɪznɪs/ 4 /ˈɑːnsə/ 5 /ˈtʃɪldrən/

Word stress

5 **a)** 3 Listen. How many syllables are there in the countries in Exercise 3a)?

Example: 1 I • ta • ly = 3 syllables

b) 4 Read the Language Box on the right. Then listen to all the words in Exercise 3a) and underline the stressed syllables in the nationalities and languages.

Sentence stress

6 5 Read the Language Box on the right. Then listen again to the sentences in Exercise 2a) and underline the syllables which have the most stress. Then listen again and repeat.

Word stress

In words of two or more syllables there is always one syllable with more stress than the others: Argentina. The vowels in unstressed syllables often have the sound /ə/ /ɑːdʒənˈtiːnə/.

Sentence stress

In English we stress important words. In every sentence there is always one word which has more stress than the others.

Example: A: Where are you from?
B: I'm from Sydney.

By the pool

Present Simple of *be: he, she, it*
Adjectives for people and places
Countable nouns: *a / an, some* and *any*
Plural nouns: regular and irregular

Present Simple of *be: he, she, it*

1 **a)** Look at the picture and read the conversation. Fill in the gaps with *'s, is* or *isn't*.

ANNA: Who's he?
JO: He's Michael. He............(1) a writer.
ANNA: Where............(2) he from?
JO: Ireland.
ANNA: Is he married?
JO: No, he isn't. He............(3) single.
ANNA: ....(4) he nice?
JO: Yes, he is. He............(5) lovely.
ANNA: And who............(6) she?
JO: She............(7) Jessica. She............(8) a dance teacher.
ANNA: Where............(9) she from?
JO: England.
ANNA: ....(10) she married?
JO: Yes, she ....(11). She............(12) married to George.
ANNA: Oh. ....(13) she nice?
JO: No, she ....(14). She............(15) awful. She............(16) very unfriendly.

b) 6 Listen and check.

Adjectives for people and places

2 Fill in the table with adjectives from the Word Box. Underline the stressed syllables.

> awful✔ OK   nice   lovely   really nice
> horrible   very unfriendly   all right

 | |
--- | --- | ---
 | | awful

Adjectives

Adjectives never change. They are never plural.
He's **nice** and they're **nice** too.
Adjectives go **before** their nouns.
They're nice people.

adjective noun

3 In pairs. Student A, look at page 124 and Student B at page 128.

4 **a)** Underline the adjectives in these sentences from two postcards. Add to your lists in Exercise 2.

Example: 1 The beach is <u>beautiful</u> and really <u>clean</u>.

2 There aren't any good nightclubs.
3 The beach is dirty. It's ten kilometres from my hotel and there isn't a good road to it.
4 The people are nice and friendly.
5 There's a lovely café and some good restaurants near my hotel.
6 The people are boring.
7 There are two shops but they're very expensive.
8 There's an interesting museum.

b) Match four sentences from Exercise 4a) to each postcard.

a) Dear . . .
It's really nice here

b) Dear . . .
It's really awful here

Countable nouns: *a / an*, *some* and *any*

5 Read the sentences from Exercise 4a) again. Then fill in the Language Box below with *a / an, some* or *any*.

> ### *A / An, some, any* and *There is / There are*
>
> **Positive sentences**
> We use .... or .... with singular nouns and .... with plural nouns.
>
> **Negative sentences**
> We use .... or .... with singular nouns and .... with plural nouns.
>
> **Look!**
> • We use *there is / isn't* with singular nouns and *there are / aren't* with plural nouns.

Plural nouns: regular and irregular

6 **a)** What is the singular of the plural nouns in the Word Box?

Example: wife (singular) → wives (plural)

> wives✓   shops   hotels   women   beaches   people
> restaurants   museums   children   countries   men

b) Make sentences with the adjectives in Exercise 2 and the nouns in Exercise 6a).

Example: There are some lovely shops.

> *Grammar reference and puzzles*
> *Be: page 102*

At reception

Checking in: alphabet, spelling,
  numbers for rooms and floors
Possessive adjectives: *my, your, our,*
  their, his, her, its
Filling in forms

Checking in

1 ▣7 A guest is checking into
the Royal Hotel. Listen. What is
the guest's name and room
number?

1 a) Cosentini b) Cosenteno
  c) Cosentena
2 a) 313 b) 343 c) 303

2 a) ▣8 Listen and repeat the
letters of the alphabet. Then fill
in the boxes.

Aa	Bb	Cc	Dd	Ee
Ff	Gg	Hh	Ii	Jj	Kk
Ll	Mm	Nn	Oo	Pp
Qq	Rr	Ss	Tt	Uu
Vv	Ww	Xx	Yy	Zz

1 /eɪ/ `a` `h` `j` `k`
2 /iː/ `b` □ □ □ □ □ □
3 /e/ `f` □ □ □ □ □
4 /uː/ `q` □ □
5 /aɪ/ `i`
6 /əʊ/ `o`
7 /ɑː/ `r`

b) ▣9 Listen and check.

3 ▣10 Listen to people
checking into the hotel. Fill in
the forms below with
surnames and room numbers.

The Royal Hotel

1 Room number .... Mr Mrs Miss (Ms) Surname .... First name(s) .... *Sarah*
2 Room number .... (Mr) (Mrs) Miss Ms Surname .... First name(s) *Richard and Patricia*
3 Room number .... (Mr) Mrs Miss Ms Surname .... First name(s) .... *John*

4 **a)** In pairs. Look at the picture of the Royal Hotel. Fill in the gaps with words and numbers from the Word Box.

| first ✓ | ground | second |
third	fifth	sixth	fourth
1st ✓	5th	3rd
2nd	4th	6th

b) 🔊 10 Listen again. Fill in the gaps. What floors are the people in Exercise 3 on?

1 She's on the .... floor.
2 They're on the .... floor.
3 He's on the .... floor.

Royal Hotel

= the ....(......) floor

= the ....(......) floor

= the ....(......) floor

= the ....(......) floor

= the ....(......) floor

= the <u>first</u> (1st) floor

= the .... floor

Possessive adjectives

5 Read the Language Box on the right. Then fill in the gaps in the sentences with *my, your, our, their, his, her* or *its*.

Example: I'm Felix. = My name's Felix.

1 You're Mr Quirk.   = ... name's Mr Quirk.
2 She's Sarah.   = ... name's Sarah.
3 He's Tom.   = ... name's Tom.
4 They're George and Jessica. = ... names are George and Jessica.
5 It's the Royal Hotel.   = ... name's the Royal Hotel.
6 We're the Thompsons.   = ... name's Thompson.

6 Student A, look at page 117 and Student B page 120.

Filling in forms

7 **a)** Look at Mr Cosentini's hotel form on the right. Fill in the gaps with the information about him from the Word Box.

| American | 1033 Wilder Avenue, San Francisco, California |
| Al Frederick | The USA | CA 94010 |

b) Write two forms like the one in Exercise 7a) in your notebook. Fill in the first form with information about you.

c) In pairs. Take it in turns to fill in your second forms with information about your partner. Then write about your partner.

Example: His surname is Binkowski. His first name is Marek. He's Polish. He's from Warsaw. His address is . . .

's = possessive or is

's = possessive
Mr Cosentini**'s** form = **his** form
Marta**'s** book = **her** book
Jo and Al**'s** drinks = **their** drinks
Look!
• Plural nouns ending in -*s*, add *'*: *the boys' room.*
• Plural nouns not ending in -*s*, add **'s**: *the men's toilets.*
's = contraction of *is*
Mr Cosentini**'s** American. = Mr Cosentini **is** American.
Marta**'s** Polish. = Marta **is** Polish.

Room number   303
Ⓜ Mr Mrs Miss Ms
Surname   Cosentini
First name(s)
Nationality
Address

Postcode
Country

11

In the café

Excuse me . . .
What's this in English?
This, these, that, those
Money and numbers: 10 to 1,000,000
What's the time?

Excuse me . . .

1 a) In pairs. Look at the picture. Where are the people? Fill in the gaps in their conversations.

b) 📼 11 Listen and check.

What's this in English?

2 a) In pairs. Take it in turns to ask about the things (a–h) in the picture.

Example: A: What's this in English?
B: It's a battery.

b) 📼 12 Look at the picture. Listen and repeat.

c) In pairs. Take it in turns to ask about two more things in the classroom.

This, these, that, those

3 In pairs. Look at the picture on page 115.

Money and numbers: 10 to 1,000,000

4 a) Fill in the gaps with numbers for these words.
Example: eleven 11

twelve .... thirteen .... fifteen ....
twenty .... forty .... fifty .... seventy ....
a / one hundred ....
a / one hundred and eighteen ....
two hundred ....
a / one thousand ....
one thousand, three hundred and ninety ....
sixty thousand ....
a / one million ....

b) 📼 13 Listen and underline the stressed syllables in Exercise 4a).

.... 's this in English?

I don't ....

It's a battery.

5 a) [oo] 14 Listen. Tick (✓) the number you hear.

1 a) 217 (two hundred and seventeen) ☐
b) 270 (two hundred and seventy) ☐
2 a) 413 (four hundred and thirteen) ☐
b) 430 (four hundred and thirty) ☐

b) [oo] 15 Now listen to the conversations and tick (✓) the number you hear.

1 a) £1.16 ☐ b) £1.60 ☐
2 a) $4,390 ☐ b) $4,319 ☐
3 a) 15,000 ☐ b) 50,000 ☐
4 a) 12,000,000 ☐ b) 20,000,000 ☐

What's the time?

6 a) Read the Language Box below. Then look at the clocks (1–8) and fill in the times in the gaps.

Telling the time			
10:00		ten o' clock.	
10:05		five	
10:15		quarter	**past** ten.
10:30	It's	half	
10:35		twenty-five	
10:45		quarter	**to** eleven.
10:55		five	

Look!
10:19 = nineteen **minutes past** ten.
10:49 = eleven **minutes to** eleven.

What's the time?

1 **8:30** It's half past eight.
2 **7:45** It's .... eight.
3 **7:50** It's .... eight.
4 **8:05** It's .... eight.
5 **7:43** It's .... eight.
6 **8:15** It's .... eight.
7 **8:25** It's .... - .... eight.
8 **8:19** It's .... eight.

b) [oo] 16 Listen and check. Then listen and repeat the times.

Look at the Word lists for Welcome A–D on pages 129–130 and check that you know all the new words.

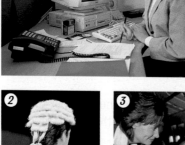

Jobs
Present Simple: *I, you, we, they*
Prepositions in time expressions
Leisure: activities and places
Skills: The Oasis Leisure Centre

Jobs

1 **a)** Look at the photographs (1–10). What do the people do? Use the words in the Word Box to make sentences.

> secretary /ˌsekrɪtəri/✓ engineer /endʒənɪə/ doctor artist
> waiter journalist /ˌdʒɜːnəlɪst/ musician
> flight attendant receptionist lawyer /ˈlɔːjə/

Example: 1 She's a secretary.

b) 🔊 17 Listen to the sentences from Exercise 1a). Underline the stressed syllables in the words for jobs. Then listen again and repeat.

Example: 1 She's a <u>se</u>cretary.

2 **a)** Ask five students about their jobs or studies. Make notes about their answers.

Example: A: What do you do?
B: I'm a receptionist. What about you?
A: I'm a student. And what do you do?
C: I don't have a job at the moment. I'm unemployed.

b) Tell the class about the people you talked to.

Example: Laura's a receptionist.

ADAM: I'm an accountant in the Accounts Department. I get up at five o'clock every morning. I always get to work early and make the coffee. There are ten people in my department and we work very hard. We don't have lunch breaks. Our bosses think meetings are important. They have meetings on Mondays and Fridays. I go to every meeting and write the reports.

Present Simple: *I, you, we, they*

Positive and negative sentences

3 **a)** Look at the Vision Design office. Is it busy? Are the people relaxed? What do Adam, John and Emma do? Read what they say and match two of the pictures (1–6) to each person.

EMMA: I speak six languages. I'm a translator and I work in the International Sales Department with two other translators. We study languages in the evenings for our jobs. I go on four business trips a month and I write reports after each trip. I sometimes go abroad on business but I don't have holidays.

JOHN: I wake up at half past five in the morning and study company reports in bed. I go to work at half past seven. I never leave the office before nine o'clock at night. I don't go out in the week because I'm too tired. I'm a manager and I read management books in my free time. I work at home at the weekend.

b) Read about Adam, John and Emma again. Underline the verbs (not *am, is, are*). Then fill in the gaps in the Language Box below.

Present Simple: *I, you, we, they*

Positive sentences	Negative sentences
JOHN: I .... management books in my free time.	**EMMA:** I .... holidays.
EMMA: We <u>study</u> languages in the evenings for our jobs.	**JOHN:** I .... out in the week.
ADAM: They .... meetings on Mondays and Fridays.	**ADAM:** We .... lunch breaks.

Look!
- We use *do* + *not* + verb in negative sentences with *I, you, we, they*.
- When we speak we usually say *don't* (contraction), not *do not*.

Questions

4 a) 👀 18 Look at the picture and advertisement above. Annie Smith wants the job at Vision Design. She's at an interview. Listen. Do you think she's the right person for the job?

b) Read the Language Box below. Then fill in the gaps in Adam's, John's and Emma's questions. Use the verbs in the Word Box.

> ### Present Simple: I, you, we, they
>
> **Yes / No questions**
> A: **Do** you **work** for a bank?
>
> A: **Do** you **work** for Vision Design?
>
> **Wh- questions**
> A: What **do** you **study**?
> A: Where **do** they **work**?
>
> **Short answers**
> B: **No, I don't.** I work for a design company.
>
> B: **Yes, I do.**
>
> **Answers**
> B: Management.
> B: At Vision Design.

work ✓   speak   do (x 2)   want   study

1 Where do you <u>work</u> now?
2 What do you .... ?
3 Do you .... any languages?
4 Do you .... in your free time?
5 What do you .... in your free time?
6 Why do you .... this job?

c) Match the answers (a–f) below to the questions (1–6) in Exercise 4b).

Example: 1 = d)

a) Because Vision Design is a good company and it's near my house.
b) No, I don't.
c) Yes, I do. I speak Spanish. I go to Spain or Latin America every year.
d) The Third Eye Design Company.
e) In the evening I watch television or listen to music. At the weekend I see my friends.
f) I'm a secretary in the Accounts Department.

5 In pairs. Student A, look at page 121 and Student B look at page 123.

Prepositions in time expressions

6 Read about Adam, John and Emma in Exercise 3a) again. Then fill in the gaps in the Language Box below.

Prepositions in time expressions

Times
...... five o'clock / half past five

Parts of the day
...... the morning / the afternoon / the evening / the night

Days
...... Monday / Wednesday

Look!
• We say **in** *the night* but .... *night*.
• We say .... *the week* but .... *the weekend*.
• There isn't a preposition before these time expressions:
every week / month / Saturday; this month / week / year; today

---

Leisure: activities and places

7 **a)** Match the activities and places in the Word Box to the photographs.

> skiing ✓   a nightclub   video games   the opera
> basketball   the theatre   a pub   horse-riding

Example: 1 = skiing

b) Do we use *go*, *go to*, or *play* with the activities and places in the Word Box in Exercise 7a)?

Example: 1 go skiing

c) Do we use *go*, *go to*, or *play* with the activities and places in the Word Box below?

> fishing ✓   golf   the cinema   tennis   cycling
> a restaurant   swimming   the ballet   volleyball

Example: go fishing

Work and play

8 **a)** In small groups. When and where do you work and play? Write at least ten *Yes / No* questions to ask the students in the other groups.

Examples: Do you work in an office?
Do you go to school / college / university?
Do you go to a bar in the evening?

b) Ask the students your questions. If the student says *Yes*, ask more questions.

Examples: A: Do you work in an office?   B: Yes, I do.
A: Where do you work?
A: What do you do?
A: Who do you work for?
A: Do you like your job?

Wavelength page

The OASIS Leisure Centre

WELCOME!

[4] Our two modern swimming pools are open every day. Beginners – learn to swim with our expert teachers. There are classes for adults on Tuesdays and Wednesdays and a class for children on Thursdays. The small second pool is for children under nine years old – so all the family can enjoy swimming.

☐ Play five-a-side football on Tuesdays and Thursdays. Men and women welcome! Bring trainers! Join the Oasis football teams, too – we play every Saturday.

☐ Use our four outdoor tennis courts and two indoor courts from Tuesday to Sunday. Book a court at reception and ask about individual and group lessons with our tennis professional, Mark. You can also hire tennis rackets and balls.

☐ Have fun and get fit. We have exercise classes for all levels with experienced and friendly teachers. The classes are on Monday and Friday evenings and Tuesday mornings.

☐ Our gym has modern equipment for all levels. Our teachers are there every day to help you develop your personal exercise programme. There are "Women only" afternoons on Wednesdays.

☐ There are yoga classes in the evenings (Monday, Tuesday and Friday) and a lunchtime class on Wednesdays. For people who want to relax and enjoy themselves at the same time.

Telephone: 01932 472 0139
for more information

---

1 Read the brochure about the Oasis Leisure Centre quickly. Match the photographs (1–6) to the paragraphs about the activities. Which activities would you like to do?

2 Fill in the gaps with words from the Word Box.

> fit ✓   beginners   exercise
> trainers /ˈtreɪnəz/   team   hire

Example: I always run to work because I want to keep fit. It's only five kilometres.

1 The eleven players in our football .... are all very good.
2 Look at you! You never do any .... You just sit in front of that TV and do nothing.
3 We can .... a bicycle for only £5 an hour.
4 I can't swim. Is there a class for .... ?
5 I always wear .... at the gym.

3 Are these sentences true or false? Write T or F in the boxes. Then correct the false sentences.

Example: There are three swimming pools.   [F]
There aren't three swimming pools. There are two.

1 Mark is the football professional.   ☐
2 There are six tennis courts.   ☐
3 Beginners can join the exercise classes.   ☐
4 There are yoga classes every day.   ☐

4 👀 19 Listen to three people asking for information and fill in the gaps.

	Time	£
1 Swimming (adults)	.... to 9 p.m.	....
2 Exercise classes	10 a.m. to	.... a class
3 Tennis	.... to	.... an hour

5 **a)** In groups of three. You have a small leisure centre in the town / city where you live. Choose five activities for your leisure centre. Make a list of the different activities, classes, times and prices.

b) Write five questions to ask other leisure centres. Go round the class and ask your questions.

Example: Are the tennis courts open on Tuesdays?

Family, friends and neighbours

Present Simple: *he, she, it*
People in your life
Frequency adverbs
Conversations: *Help!*

Present Simple: *he, she, it*

Positive and negative sentences

1 **a)** Nickie Griffin is from South Africa, but she lives and works in London. Read the beginning of her letter to her parents. Is she happy in London?

b) Are these sentences true (T) or false (F)?

1 Nickie works for Vision Design.
2 Carol the receptionist is very nice.
3 Mike's an engineer.
4 Mike, Sarah and Leo live next door.

c) Read Nickie's letter again and underline the positive Present Simple verbs (not *am, is, are*). Then fill in the table.

Example: He <u>works</u> for the BBC and <u>goes</u> abroad a lot.

I / we / you / they	he / she / it
go	goes
have	
invite	
live	
love	
play	
say	
speak	
stay	
study	
talk	
teach	
watch	
work	works

47 Dove Street
London N1

17th March

Dear Mum and Dad,

Thanks for your letter. I'm glad everybody is OK.

Life's great at the moment because I have a new job with a company called Vision Design. It's really interesting and the people I work with are a lot of fun — except the receptionist, Carol. She's a bit strange. Eve, the boss, is really nice. Sometimes after work I go to a pub or a restaurant with them. I work very long hours — but that's life. I love London now, but it's very different from Cape Town. It's so fast.

I live with Pat, a friend from work. She's great. She's a designer. Here's a photo of us in her beautiful flat.

Some of the neighbours are really nice. There's a family upstairs, who are very friendly. Mike, the husband, is a journalist. He works for the BBC and goes abroad a lot. His wife, Sarah, plays the piano and studies music. She teaches the piano in the evenings. Their son, Leo, plays the piano too. He's only four years old but he plays Mozart! Sarah sometimes invites me round for dinner when Mike's abroad and we talk for hours.

But the woman in the flat next door — Mrs Jackson — is awful. I always say "hello" to her but she doesn't speak to me. She just stays in her flat and watches TV.

2 a) There is one negative sentence in Nickie's letter on page 19. Find it and fill in the gaps in the Language Box on the right.

b) In pairs. Take it in turns to correct these sentences.

Example: A: Nickie works for a bank.
B: No, she doesn't work for a bank. She works for a design company.

1 Nickie goes to the theatre after work.   5 Mike stays in England.
2 Nickie lives with Eve.   6 Sarah teaches English.
3 Pat has a beautiful house.   7 Sarah's son plays the guitar.
4 Mike works for CNN.

3 Look at the photographs on the right and read the rest of Nickie's letter. Fill in the gaps with the correct form of the verbs in the Word Box.

| rush ✓ | have (x 2) | want | talk | say | see |
| study | stop | like | work (x 2) | not like | |

Two South Africans live downstairs – Jenny and Jim. They're brother and sister. Jenny's always in a hurry – she ......rushes......... everywhere! She's a waitress – she ....(1) her job! She ....(2) it's very boring. She ....(3) very hard and she's always tired. Jim ....(4) medicine. He ....(5) to be a doctor. I don't see Jenny a lot because she ....(6) in the evenings and she ....(7) a boyfriend, Harry. I think Jim ....(8) me. He always ....(9) and ....(10) to me when he ....(11) me on the stairs. But he ....(12) a girlfriend, Emily . . .

How's my little brother Ian? What time does he get up these days – lunchtime? Does he listen to music all day?

Lots of love,

Nickie

The Griffin family

Questions and answers

4 a) Look at the end of Nickie's letter again and fill in the gaps in the Language Box on the right.

b) Now make questions for these answers.

Example: What does Sarah teach?   The piano.

1 She's a designer.   2 Upstairs.   3 South Africa.   4 Medicine.

c) In pairs. Make questions and answer them.

Example: Mike / go abroad a lot?
A: Does Mike go abroad a lot?   B: Yes, he does.

1 Nickie / work for a design company?   3 Jim / live with his brother?
2 Mrs Jackson / speak to Nickie?   4 Jenny / work very hard?

Present Simple: he, she, it

Negative sentences
She .... to me.
We use *doesn't* (does + not) + verb in negative sentences with *he, she, it.*
When we speak we usually say *doesn't* (contraction), not *does not.*

Present Simple: he, she, it

Wh- questions
What time .... he .... up?
Answers
At twelve o'clock.
Yes / No questions
.... he .... to music all day?
Short answers
Yes, he does. / No, he doesn't.

Mike, Sarah and Leo

Harry and Jenny, Emily and Jim

Eve and Nickie

Pronunciation: *does*

5 a) 🎧 20 Listen. Is *does* stressed /dʌz/ or weak /dəz/? Write S (stressed) or W (weak) in the boxes.

Examples: Does /dəz/ ☒W Leo play the piano?
Yes, he does /dʌz/ ☒S.

1 Where does ☐ he live?
2 Does ☐ he like her?
3 Yes, he does ☐.
4 What does ☐ she do?
5 Does ☐ she work in a bank?
6 Yes, she does ☐.

b) 🎧 20 Listen again and underline the main stressed syllable in each sentence. Then listen again and repeat.

Examples: Does Leo play the pi<u>a</u>no?
Yes, he <u>does</u>.

6 In pairs. Look at the people (1–12) in the photographs (a–d). Use the words in the Word Box and say who they are.

> father   husband   wife   mother   neighbour   brother
> friend   sister   boss   boyfriend   son   girlfriend   daughter

Example: 1 Mr Griffin is Nickie and Ian's father and Mrs Griffin's husband.

Pronunciation: /s/, /z/ and /ɪz/

7 🎧 21 Listen. Is the sound at the end of these words 1 /s/, 2 /z/ or 3 /ɪz/? Fill in the boxes. Then listen again and repeat.

Examples: works /s/ ☐1
does /z/ ☐2
watches /ɪz/ ☐3

1 lives ☐   6 invites ☐
2 Sarah's ☐   7 She's ☐
3 He's ☐   8 says ☐
4 stays ☐   9 Nickie's ☐
5 talks ☐   10 stops ☐

People in your life

8 a) Make a list of four important people in your life.

b) In groups of four. Take it in turns to ask and answer questions about the people. Ask *Yes / No* questions first. Then ask *Wh-* questions to find out more information.

Example: A: Who's important in your life?   B: My brother.
A: Does your brother work?   B: No, he doesn't.
A: What does he do in his leisure time?   B: He listens to music.
A: What kind of music does he like?   B: Pop music.

Frequency adverbs

9 a) Look at these answers to the question. Which is your answer?

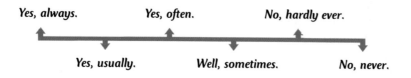

Do you work at the weekend?

Yes, always.   **Yes, often.**   **No, hardly ever.**

Yes, usually.   **Well, sometimes.**   **No, never.**

b) 👀 22 Listen and repeat the answers. Then ask four people the question.

10 a) 👀 23 Look at the picture of Carol, the receptionist at Vision Design. Nickie and a friend are talking about her. Listen. Do you think they like her? Do you think Carol likes her job? Fill in the gaps with words from the Word Box.

> often   always   hardly ever   sometimes   never   usually

Example: smoke / in reception often

1 phone / friends from work ....
2 take / long coffee breaks ....
3 give / messages ....
4 argue / with the boss ....
5 smile ....
6 be / late in the morning ....

b) Look at the Language Box on the right and write complete sentences for (1–6) from Exercise 10a).

Example: She often smokes in reception.

Do you ever . . . ? How often do you . . . ?

11 In groups. How do you feel about your job or studies? Ask and answer these questions.

Examples: argue with your colleagues / teacher / boss / classmates
  A: Do you ever argue with your colleagues?
  B: Yes, sometimes. One woman is really awful.

  take time off
  C: How often do you take time off?
  D: Hardly ever.

1 have problems at work / school / college / university
2 leave early
3 arrive late
4 enjoy your work / studies
5 get angry / stressed / bored
6 have problems at home / with your family

Frequency adverbs in sentences

Frequency adverbs come **before** main verbs but **after** *be*.

Carol **often smokes** in reception.
Carol **is often** late.

Grammar reference and puzzles
Present Simple: page 103

22

Conversations *Help!*

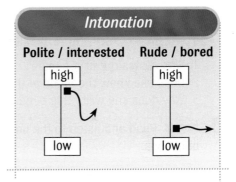

Phoning a hotel

1 a) 🔊 24 Look at the photograph. Carlos Garcia is a businessman. He's in London on a business trip. He's phoning a hotel. Listen and read the conversation. Where is he?

RECEPTIONIST: ...., Majestic Hotel. How may I help you?

CARLOS: .... Carlos Garcia. I have a reservation for tonight but . . .

RECEPTIONIST: .... I can't hear you. Could .... ?

CARLOS: Oh, um, ... Mr Garcia, Carlos Garcia. G–A–R–C–I–A.

RECEPTIONIST: Yes, Mr Garcia. We have a reservation for you.

CARLOS: I'm at the airport at the moment. And I don't have the address of the hotel.

RECEPTIONIST: It's 34 Wesley Street.

CARLOS: 34, um, sorry, this .... Could .... ?

RECEPTIONIST: Yes, it's 34 Wesley Street. That's W–E–S–L–E–Y Street.

CARLOS: Thank you very much.

b) 🔊 24 Listen again and fill in the gaps.

Pronunciation: intonation

2 a) 🔊 25 Look at the Language Box on the right. Then listen to the receptionists. Which receptionists are polite and interested? Which receptionists are rude and bored? Put a tick (✓) for polite and interested and a cross (✗) for rude and bored.

Examples: a) ✓ b) ✗

1 a) ☐ b) ☐   2 a) ☐ b) ☐   3 a) ☐ b) ☐

b) 🔊 26 In pairs. Listen to the polite receptionists and repeat.

c) In pairs. Student A, look at page 117 and Student B at page 123.

Signs

3 In pairs. Look at the picture. What is in the boxes? What do you think Fred and Sam are talking about? Can you fill in the gaps in their conversation?

FRED: Excuse me.

SAM: Yes?

FRED: What does this .... ?

SAM: Oh, uh, I don't ....

4 In pairs. Student A, look at page 116 and Student B at page 120.

Wavelength page

23

Reading for pleasure

① He-mail, she-mail

Your *Wavelength Elementary* Coursebook has a Reader called *On the same wavelength and other stories* in the back. The first story is "He-mail, she-mail". Do the exercises on this page to help you understand and enjoy it.

1 Before you read the story, look at the title and answer these questions.

1 Do you use a computer? Where? What for?
2 Do you use the Internet? Where? What for?
3 Do you use e-mail? Where? What for?

2 🔊 27 Read and listen to the first part of the story. Then answer the questions.

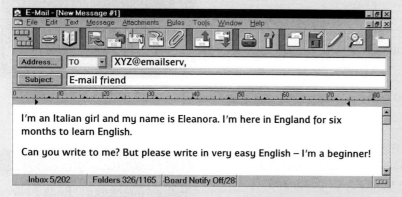

1 Who writes the first e-mail?
2 Does she know the name of the person she writes to?
3 Why does she write this e-mail?

3 🔊 28 Read and listen to the next part of the story. Then answer the questions.

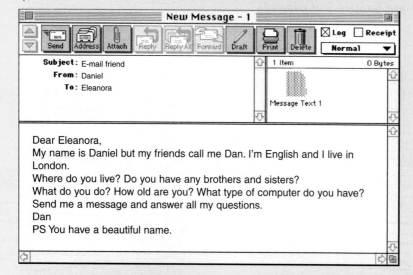

1 Who answers Eleanora's e-mail?
2 Does he know Eleanora?
3 Why does he answer her e-mail?

4 Read the two e-mails again. Are these sentences true (T) or false (F)? Correct the false sentences.

Example: Eleanora is Italian. [T]
She's in Italy at the moment. [F]
She isn't in Italy at the moment. She's in England.

1 She's in England for a year. ☐
2 She knows a lot of English. ☐
3 Dan is English. ☐
4 He asks Eleanora a lot of questions. ☐
5 He likes her name. ☐

5 Now read the whole story. It starts on page 2 of *On the same wavelength and other stories*. What happens when Eleanora and Dan e-mail each other? Think about these questions while you read.

1 Is Eleanora's family rich? Why do you think that?
2 Is Dan's family rich? Why do you think that?
3 Why is Eleanora in England?
4 Is Dan a student or does he have a job?
5 Look at the subjects at the top of each e-mail. Are they important?
6 Is "He-mail, she-mail" an adventure story, a crime story, a love story or a comedy?

Lifestyles

Love and *hate*
Can / can't for ability
Day to day English: Offers

Love and *hate*

1 **a)** Look at the pictures (a–e). Where is Jane in each picture? Does she look happy?

b) 🎧 29 Listen. Jane's talking to friends about what she likes and doesn't like. Match the conversations to the pictures.
1 [e] 2 ☐ 3 ☐ 4 ☐ 5 ☐

2 🎧 29 How does Jane feel about these things (a–f)? Listen again and make sentences. Then read the Language Box on the right.

Example: 1 = d)

1 She loves	a) warm weather.
2 She really likes	b) flying.
3 She likes	c) lying on a beach.
4 She doesn't mind	d) football.
5 She doesn't like	e) the new boss.
6 She hates	f) the new café.

Love / like / don't mind / hate

After some verbs (*love, like, don't / doesn't mind, hate*) we can use a noun, a pronoun or a verb + *-ing*.

I **love** planes. ⎫
I **hate** football. ⎬ noun

I **love** them. ⎫
I **hate** it. ⎬ pronoun

I **love** flying. ⎫
I **hate** watching ⎬ verb + *-ing*
football. ⎭

3 What is the spelling of the *-ing* form? Fill in the gaps in the Language Box on the right.

4 **a)** Make sentences about yourself with the verbs in the Word Box.

> love   really like   like   don't mind   don't like   hate

Examples: I love shopping.
   I hate writing letters.

b) In pairs. Compare your sentences.

5 🔊 30 Read the questionnaire. Then listen to Jane and Bob and fill in the questionnaire for Bob. Write B (Bob).

Spelling of the *-ing* form

- Verb + *-ing*: study → study**ing**, fly → .... , talk → ....
- Verbs ending in *-e* take off the *-e*: come → com**ing**, write → .... BUT *be* → *being*.
- Verbs ending in a vowel + a consonant, double the consonant: swim → swim**ming**, shop → ....

THE REAL YOU!

WHAT ARE YOU REALLY LIKE?
DO OUR SIMPLE QUESTIONNAIRE TO FIND OUT!

ARE YOU A "PEOPLE PERSON" OR A LONER?

Do you like . . .	love	really like	like	don't mind	don't like	hate
1 talking to friends?	B					
2 going out with friends?						
3 spending time alone?						
4 meeting new people?						
5 going on holiday alone?						
6 going to parties?						
7 staying at home?						

DO YOU LOOK AFTER YOURSELF?

Do you like . . .	love	really like	like	don't mind	don't like	hate
1 doing sports?						
2 going for walks?						
3 watching TV?						
4 active holidays?						
5 relaxing on holiday?						
6 healthy food?						
7 smoking?						

6 a) ⟦oo⟧31 Listen again to some of Jane's questions and Bob's answers. Fill in the gaps.

Example: JANE: <u>Do you like</u> talking to friends?
BOB: Yes, I love <u>it.</u>

1 JANE: .... going out with friends?
BOB: Yeah, I ....
2 JANE: .... going on holiday alone?
BOB: Oh, yes, I really like ....
3 JANE: .... doing sports?
BOB: No, I ....
4 JANE: .... watching TV?
BOB: Well, I don't mind ....
5 JANE: .... active holidays?
BOB: No, I hate <u>them.</u>

b) ⟦oo⟧32 Listen and repeat the answers. Underline the main stressed syllables in the answers in Exercise 6a).

Example: Yes, I <u>love</u> it.

7 a) In pairs. Look at the questionnaire in Exercise 5 again. Take it in turns to ask and answer the questions. Fill in the questionnaire for your partner.

b) What kind of people are Bob and your partner? Look at page 126 to find out.

Can / can't for ability: Mr Perfect

8 What can Roger do? Match the sentences (1–5) to the pictures (a–e).

Example: 1 He can play the violin. = c)

2 He can speak Arabic.   4 He can play tennis.
3 He can sing.   5 He can paint.

9 ⟦oo⟧33 Listen. Jane, Bob and Nadia are having dinner. Roger works in their office. They're talking about him. Do they all like him?

10 a) 🎧33 Listen again and fill in the boxes.
Tick (✓) the things that Jane says to Bob.
Put a cross (✗) by the things she doesn't say.

Example: You can't play the violin. ✓

1 You can't play tennis. ☐
2 You can't sing. ☐
3 You can't paint. ☐
4 You can't speak Italian. ☐
5 You can't speak Arabic. ☐

b) 🎧33 Listen again and fill in the gaps.

JANE: Roger .can... .... languages.
What languages .... , Bob?
BOB: Well . . . I .... Italian.
JANE: No, you .... You .... Italian.
BOB: Yes, I ....

11 Fill in the gaps in the Language Box on the right.

Pronunciation: *can* and *can't*

12 🎧34 Listen. Which sound do you hear? Write 1 /kən/, 2 /kæn/ or
3 /kɑːnt/ in the boxes. Then listen again and repeat.

Examples: I can /kən/ ① swim. Can /kən/ ① she swim?
Yes, she can /kæn/ ② .
He can't /kɑːnt/ ③ swim.

1 Can ☐ he play tennis?
2 Yes, he can ☐ .
3 They can't ☐ sing.
4 What languages can ☐ she speak?
5 Can ☐ she paint?
6 No, she can't ☐ .
7 I can ☐ speak Japanese.
8 I can't ☐ speak Portuguese.

What can you do?

13 In pairs. Write four questions to ask your partner. Then take it in
turns to ask and answer questions. Ask about friends and family too.

Examples: A: Can you play the piano?
B: No, I can't – but I can play the guitar.
A: Can you play well?
B: Yes, I can. I sometimes play with my friends.
A: . . .

Can / can't

Positive

Subject		Verb
I / You / We / They / He / She / It	....	sing.

Negative

Subject		Verb
I / You / We / They / He / She / It	....	sing.

Questions and answers

A: .... you speak Spanish?
B: Yes, I .... / No, I ....
A: .... he speak German?
B: Yes, he .... / No, he ....
A: What language .... he speak?
B: Polish.

Look!

• Contractions: *can't* = *cannot* (one word)

Day to day English *Offers*

Looking after guests

Saying *Yes* and *No* to offers

1 **a)** Paolo is in England on business. He's with his boss, Gerald, and Gerald's wife, Mary, at their house. Match Mary's questions with Paolo's answers.

Example: 1 = b)

Mary's questions	Paolo's answers
1 How are you? Good journey?	a) No, thank you. I don't smoke.
2 Would you like something to drink? Some tea or coffee?	b) Yes. Fine, thank you.
3 Would you like a snack too?	c) Ham, please.
4 What about a sandwich?	d) Oh, yes. Tea, please.
5 Would you like cheese or ham?	e) Oh, yes, please. A sandwich sounds good.
6 Would you like a cigarette?	f) OK, thank you. Just something small, please.

b) 🎧 35 Listen and check. Then read the Language Box below.

> ### Drinks
>
> We can talk about drinks in two ways – with *some* or with *a / an* (= a glass of / a cup of . . .)
>
> I'd like *some* orange juice.
> OR
> I'd like *a* coffee.
>
> Would you like *an* orange juice?
> OR
> Would you like *some* coffee?

2 **a)** 🎧 36 Listen and repeat Mary's offers and Paolo's answers. How do they pronounce *would you* /ˈwʊdʒə/, *some* /səm/ and *a* /ə/?

b) In pairs. Practise the conversation.

3 We usually give a reason when we say *No*. Match the questions to the answers.

Example: 1 = d)

Questions
1 Would you like a cigarette?
2 Would you like something to eat?
3 Would you like something to drink?
4 Would you like a beer?

Answers
a) No, thanks. I'm not thirsty at the moment.
b) No, thanks. I don't drink.
c) No, thanks. I'm not hungry.
d) No, thanks. I don't smoke.

4 All students, look at page 125.

Secrets and lies

Present Continuous: now

1 a) Read the questionnaire. Then write one more question for it.

b) Go round the class and talk to two students. Take it in turns to ask and answer the questions and fill in the questionnaire.

2 a) [oo] 37 Look at the photograph of Polly and Pete. What are they doing? Listen to Pete's telephone conversation with Rob and answer the questions.

1 Does Polly want to speak to Rob?
2 What does Pete say about Polly?
3 Is this true? What is Polly really doing?

b) [oo] 37 Listen again and fill in the gaps.

PETE: Hello?
ROB: Hi. .... Rob.
PETE: Oh hi, Rob.
ROB: .... Polly .... ?
PETE: Er, yeah.
ROB: Oh. Is she .... ?
PETE: No, she isn't, but she's .... a shower. Can I .... a message?
ROB: Um, yeah. Can she .... me this evening?
PETE: Yeah, sure.
ROB: .... a lot.
PETE: That's .... Bye.
ROB: Bye.

c) [oo] 38 Listen and repeat. Then in pairs practise the conversation.

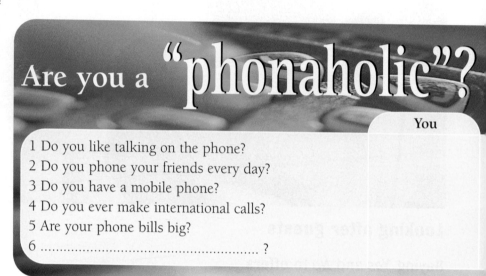

Are you a "phonaholic"?

	You
1 Do you like talking on the phone?	
2 Do you phone your friends every day?	
3 Do you have a mobile phone?	
4 Do you ever make international calls?	
5 Are your phone bills big?	
6 .... ?	

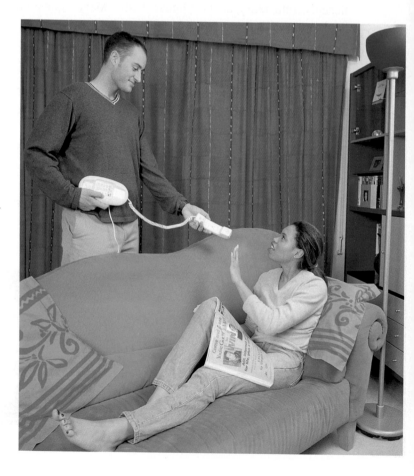

Student A   **Student B**

3 **a)** Read the conversations and fill in the gaps with words from the Word Box.

| we're | they're | I'm | having | playing | reading |

1 **MAN:** Hello, can I speak to Mr or Mrs White?
  GIRL: I'm sorry, ... tennis. Can I take a message?

2 **CAROL:** Hello, Nickie. It's Carol.
  NICKIE: Hi, Carol. I'm really sorry but my brother's here and ....
  .... dinner. Can I phone you back?
  CAROL: Yeah, that's fine.

3 **POLLY:** Hello?
  ROB: Hi, Polly. It's Rob.
  POLLY: Oh hi. What are you doing? Are you working?
  ROB: No, I'm not working. .... a magazine.

b) 🔊 39 Listen and check.

4 Now fill in the gaps in the Language Box below.

Present Continuous

We use *be* (*am / are / is*) and verb + *-ing*

Positive sentences

I	....	
You / We / They	....	working.
He / She / It	....	

Negative sentences

I	....	
You / We / They	're not	working.
He / She / It	....	

5 Make Present Continuous questions and answers.

Example: A: You / work?   B: Yes
           A: Are you working?   B: Yes, I am.

1 A: What / you / do?   B: We / talk
2 A: They / listen to music?   B: No
3 A: What / she / read?   B: She / read / a magazine
4 A: Roger / play tennis?   B: Yes

6 In pairs. Ask and answer questions about your family, colleagues and friends. Use the Present Continuous.

Example: A: What's your father doing at the moment?
           B: He's working.

7 Look at the photograph on the left of Pete and fill in the gaps in the Language Box below.

Present Simple or Present Continuous?

Pete's a lawyer. He works in the city.
= Present .... (regular habits and routines)
He **isn't working** now. He's relaxing at home.
= Present .... (now)

Hello, Mr Smith

8 **a)** Look at these pictures. What is happening? What are the people doing? Write as many Present Continuous sentences as you can about the pictures.

Examples: A The children are fighting.
The babysitter's boyfriend is watching TV.

b) 🔊 40 Listen to the phone conversations and answer the questions.

1 Who are the people talking to?
2 Are they telling the truth? What are they saying? Finish their sentences.

A The children are sleeping.
I'm ....
....

B He's ....
....

C I'm ....
....

I'm ....
....

The sun's ....
....

D I'm ....
....

3 Now tell the truth. Make sentences (A–D) negative.

Example: A The children <u>aren't</u> <u>sleeping</u>.

33 Ocean Drive
Perth
20th May

Dear Eve,

Thanks for your letter. I'm glad to hear that you and your family are all happy and successful.

Well, life's good here, too. We're all fine and I'm really enjoying life in Australia. We're living in a beautiful house near the sea. It's lovely!

Sid's new job is great. He likes the new design company. He's working really hard in the evenings at the moment. He isn't at home very much.

Jack's working for a bank now. He's having a good time and meeting some very interesting people and Judy's going out with a very nice young man.

What about me? Well, I'm not working. I'm just staying at home and looking after the house and the family.

That's all for now.

Love,

Molly

PS I'm only smoking one or two cigarettes a day!

Present Continuous: around now

9 a) Molly is from England, but she's living in Australia at the moment. Look at the pictures and read her letter to her friend, Eve, in England. Is Molly telling the truth?

b) Look at the Language Box on the right. Then find the five lies in Molly's letter. Use the words in the Word Box and make true sentences.

| worry ✓ | gamble | rob | go out | smoke |

Example: 1 Molly isn't enjoying life in Australia. She's worrying about her family.

My wonderful life!

10 a) Molly isn't happy, but she tells Eve she is. Make notes about your "wonderful life" these days. Think about work, friends, family, studies, leisure time, love life, money.

Example: 1 I'm working for an international company and making £1,000,000 a year!

b) In pairs. Have a conversation about your "wonderful lives". Begin like this.

A: Hi. How are you?
A: I'm fine. What are you doing these days?
B: I'm fine. What about you?
B: Well, I'm working . . .

Present Continuous

What is happening **around now**?

Molly's worrying.

PAST ← *at the moment* now → FUTURE

at the moment = exactly now or around now

Grammar reference and puzzles
Present Continuous: page 104

Wavelength page

1 What's the question?

In two groups. Play a question and answer game. Group A, look at page 125 and Group B at Page 127.

2 Lifestyles and leisure

In pairs. Student A, look at page 124 and Student B, look at page 126.

3 Usually or now?

a) In groups of four. Look at the pictures (1–4). What are they doing?

b) Work together and match your descriptions to the men. Student A, look at page 125; Student B at page 127; Student C at page 120 and Student D at page 123.

c) Make similar sentences about yourself. What do you usually do? What are you doing now?

4 What do you say?

Look at these three situations. What are the people saying? Fill in the gaps. Then in pairs practise one conversation.

Look at the Word lists for Units 1–4 on pages 131–133 and check that you know all the new words.

Reading for pleasure

On the same
Wavelength
and other stories

② Lost opportunities

1 Before you read the story, look at the title and the photographs and answer these questions.

1 Is the year 1812, 1912 or 1992?
2 Do you think the story has a happy ending?

2 🎧 41 Read and listen to a), the first part of the story. Then answer the questions.

1 What does Harriet do?
2 Why is she talking to the two men?
3 What does she lie about?
4 Do you think she takes the job?

3 🎧 42 Read and listen to b), another part of the story. Then answer the questions.

1 Who is Edward talking to?
2 Is the news from New York good or bad?
3 Do you think that Edward says *Yes* to Mr Harding's offer?

4 🎧 43 Read and listen to c), another part of the story. Then answer the questions.

1 Do you think that Frederick and Edith are married?
2 Why do you think Edith can't go away with Frederick?

5 Now read the whole story. It starts on page 6 of *On the same wavelength and other stories*. What happens next? Think about these questions while you read.

1 Where is Harriet's new job?
2 Where is Edward's new job?
3 When does he arrive in New York?
4 Do you think Edith loves Frederick?
5 Is Harriet's father happy about her new job?
6 Do you think her mother wants her to go?
7 How does Harriet feel after she speaks to her father?
8 Why doesn't Edward's mother want him to leave on Wednesday?
9 What is Edward's job?
10 When does Edward's mother want him to leave?
11 How does Edward feel?
12 Who is Frederick's letter from?
13 How does he feel when he reads the letter?
14 Who leaves on the ship?

(a) Harriet Frazer is at the piano.

". . . goodbye, my love . . . goodbye!" she sings.

Then she waits. This is her big chance.

"Good – very good," says one of the men.

"Well, Moss?" says the other man. His name is Coe and he is American.

"This is our girl! But she's very young . . ."

"How old are you, Miss Frazer?" asks Coe.

"I'm twenty-four." It's not true. Harriet is eighteen. Coe looks at Moss. He knows that it's a lie.

"What do you say, Miss Frazer? Are you ready to leave?" he asks.

(b)

Edward is in his boss's office.

"Ah, Edward! I have some very good news. This is a message from our New York office."

"Oh," says Edward. He is very excited. Is this his big chance? His chance of a lifetime?

"They like your work. They want to meet you."

"That's wonderful, Mr Harding," says Edward. "I'm . . . very happy."

"Well, Edward?" asks Mr Harding. "Are you ready to leave?"

(c)

Frederick is in the park.

"Edith, darling," he says. "Come away with me. I have some money from my mother. We have the chance to go away together. We can go to Paris, or to Rome. It's spring . . . and I love you."

"Sweet Frederick . . . it's a lovely idea, but I can't possibly. You know I can't."

5 You are what you wear

Clothes
Have got / has got and *have / has*
Day to day English: Permission

Clothes

1 **a)** 🎧 44 Look at the pictures. Do you like any of the clothes? Listen and match the conversations (1–4) to the pictures (A–D).

Example: 1 = D

b) In pairs. Match the clothes (a–u) to the words in the Word Box.

Example: a) = dress

> dress ✓ trousers /ˈtraʊzəz/ jacket trainers jumper
> hat sweatshirt /ˈswetʃɜːt/ sandals shoes coat
> pyjamas /pəˈdʒɑːməz/ suit /suːt/ swimsuit jeans tie
> boots shirt shorts skirt socks T-shirt

c) Some clothes are singular (*a dress*) and some are plural (*trousers*). Look at the words in the Word Box in Exercise 1b) again. Are they singular or plural? Make two lists. Then read the Language Box on the right.

d) In groups of three. Talk about your clothes. Ask and answer questions about all the plural clothes in Exercise 1b).

Example: A: How many pairs of trainers do you have?
B: I have three pairs.
C: I don't have any.

e) What are the people in the pictures on page 36 wearing? Read the Language Box on the right. Then make sentences for pictures (A–D).

2 a) In pairs. Look at the photographs of people in a clothes shop. What are they saying? Match the photographs (a–e) to the conversations (1–5).

1 ☐ A: How is it?
    B: It's fine. I'll take it.
2 ☐ A: Yes, we do. Would you like to try it?
    B: Yes, please.
3 [a] A: Can I help you?
    C: No, thanks. I'm just looking.
4 ☐ A: How are you paying?
    B: Do you take Visa?
    A: Yes, we do. That's £29.99. Thank you.
    B: Thank you.
5 ☐ B: Excuse me. Do you have this T-shirt in black?
    A: I'll have a look.

b) 🎧 45 Listen and check. Then in groups of three practise the conversations.

Plural clothes

We can say:
trousers OR **a pair of** trousers
shoes OR **a pair of** shoes

Wear or carry?

In Picture B, the man's **wearing** a T-shirt and shorts. He's **carrying** a bag. One woman's **wearing** a swimsuit.

3 a) Fill in the word map with words from the Word Box. Add more words if you can.

light blue ✓ cotton ✓ by cheque ✓ small ✓ dark blue yellow
in cash black medium red beige /beɪʒ/ by credit card
wool pink large brown white silk green

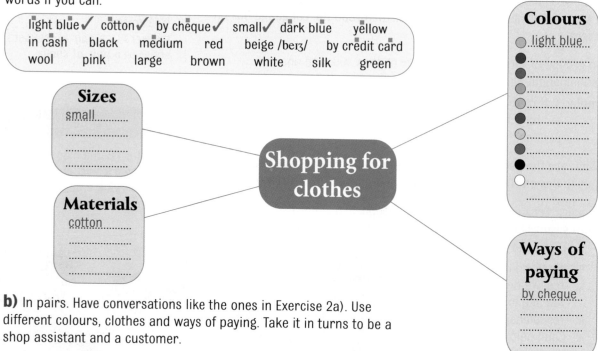

Sizes
small

Materials
cotton

Shopping for clothes

Colours
light blue

Ways of paying
by cheque

b) In pairs. Have conversations like the ones in Exercise 2a). Use different colours, clothes and ways of paying. Take it in turns to be a shop assistant and a customer.

4 In pairs. Are you a fashion victim or a slob? Do the Fashion Maze opposite and find out!

5 a) Read the Language Box on the right. Then in groups. Write five questions about fashion and clothes. Use these ideas to help you.

b) In pairs. Have a conversation. Ask your five questions from Exercise 5a) and take notes. Then answer your partner's questions.

c) Write what your partner said on a piece of paper. Don't write his / her name. Then work in groups and read the papers. Guess who they are about.

Example: A: He doesn't spend a lot of money on clothes and he hates shopping for clothes.
B: Is it Sergei?

Have got / has got and have / has

When we talk about possessions, things and people, we can use *have got / has got* or *have / has.*

Have got / has got
I**'ve got** a blue suit.
I **haven't got** a brown suit.
He**'s got** two children.
He **hasn't got** any children.

Have / has
I **have** a blue suit.
I **don't have** a brown suit.
He **has** two children.
He **doesn't have** any children.

Grammar reference and puzzles
Have got / has got and *have / has:*
page 105

The Fashion Maze
The questionnaire that doesn't lie!

1 You win £2,000,000. Do you spend it all on clothes?

Yes Go to **2** **No** Go to **3**

2 Do you buy smart, expensive clothes for your cat or dog?

Yes Go to **5** **No** Go to **6**

3 Do you spend a lot (not all) of the £2,000,000 on clothes?

Yes Go to **2** **No** Go to **11**

4 You are a fashion victim. Go to a doctor and ask for help. Or marry someone very rich.

5 A fashion magazine says that you must wear a purple, plastic swimsuit on the beach this summer. Do you wear one?

Yes Go to **7** **No** Go to **6**

6 Do you wear fashionable clothes every day?

Yes Go to **7** **No** Go to **11**

7 Do you think the name on the label is more important than the clothes?

Yes Go to **8** **No** Go to **9**

8 Your favourite designer makes plastic shorts and plastic masks this year – do you wear them to the disco?

Yes Go to **4** **No** Go to **19**

9 Giorgio Armani is a . . .

footballer Go to **14** **designer** Go to **17**

10 How often do you buy clothes?

Once a year Go to **18** **Twice a year** Go to **15** **Once a month** Go to **19**

11 Do you have any smart, fashionable clothes?

Yes Go to **9** **No** Go to **12**

12 Do you still wear that old Mickey Mouse T-shirt that you bought ten years ago?

Yes Go to **13** **No** Go to **17**

13 Do you have big holes in your socks? (Be honest!)

Yes Go to **18** **No** Go to **10**

14 When you go into a clothes shop, do the shop assistants laugh at you?

Yes Go to **10** **No** Go to **16**

15 You like fashion but you normally wear what is comfortable. Buy something fashionable. Try a new style.

16 Your boy / girlfriend goes on holiday for a week. Do you wear the same old jeans and T-shirt every day?

Yes Go to **17** **No** Go to **15**

17 Is your boy / girlfriend's opinion about your clothes important to you?

Yes Go to **20** **No** Go to **15**

18 You're a slob! You don't care about clothes at all! Go and buy some new clothes today!

19 You buy a lot of clothes, but not only because of fashion. You are a) very rich or b) very cold.

20 Don't wear clothes for other people. Wear clothes that you want to wear!

Hi, Paul. Can I watch the news?

Sorry, I'm watching the football.

Can I use your phone?

Sure, go ahead.

CHOCOLATE

DICTIONARY

Can I . . . ?

1 **a)** Paul and Jill are friends. Where are they? What does Jill want? Which answer means, *Yes, you can do that*? Which answer means, *No, you can't do that*?

b) ⊙⊙ 46 Listen and repeat.

2 **a)** Find the nouns in the picture.

Example: 1 = window

Nouns	Verbs
apples	borrow
camera	have
chocolate	listen to
computer	look at
dictionary	open / shut
door	play
guitar	read
light	turn down / turn up
magazines	turn off / turn on
money	use
personal stereo	watch
TV	
window	

b) Match the verbs to the nouns in Exercise 2a).

Example: 1 window: open / shut

3 In pairs. Imagine you're in Paul's room. Take it in turns to ask for and give / refuse permission. If you don't give permission, give a reason.

Examples: A: Can I have an apple?
B: Sure.
A: Thanks.
B: Can I listen to some music?
A: Well, sorry I'm trying to work.
B: Oh, OK.

4 In pairs. Look at page 127.

Have we got news for you!

Past Simple of regular verbs
Past Simple of irregular verbs
Time expressions for the past
Conversations: *Oh, really?*

Past Simple of regular verbs

Positive sentences

1 Do you read a newspaper, watch the news on TV or listen to the radio?

2 a) In pairs. Match the TV pictures (a–c) to the headlines (1–3).

b) Match the nouns and verbs to the TV pictures (a–c).

Nouns	Verbs
A the emergency services mobile phone	destroy escape jump die arrive phone arrest
B wedding boxer relationship	marry invite divorce start
C victory match	surprise play score injure

c) [oo] 47 Listen to the news stories and check.

d) Write the Past Simple of the regular verbs in Exercise 2b).

Examples: destroy → destroyed
marry → married
surprise → surprised

Tonight's headlines:

① Hollywood actress, Claudia Campbell, married her teenage musician boyfriend.

② A man died in a London fire.

③ And why Walden United football fans love their new star.

Negative sentences and questions

3 Look at the pictures below and read the two conversations. Then fill in the gaps in the Language Box below.

Did he phone Max?

No, he didn't.

He didn't phone Max.

Who did he phone?

Past Simple of regular verbs

Questions
We use .... + verb to make questions.

Negative sentences
We use .... + verb to make negative sentences.

---

4 Make negative sentences.

Example: The young woman phoned the emergency services. She <u>didn't phone</u> the hospital.

1 The police arrested a man this morning. They .... him last night.
2 Claudia married Eddie last night. She .... Bruno.
3 Claudia invited friends to the wedding. She .... the media.
4 Andy Dixon scored two goals in the match. He .... three.

5 a) Write questions about the stories in Exercise 2.

Examples: a) the / woman / Who / phone / did ?
Who did the woman phone?

b) Did / house / the / destroy / fire / the ?
Did the fire destroy the house?

1 fire / happen / the / did / When ?
2 hotel / the / destroy / fire / the / Did ?
3 her / did / boyfriend / When / Claudia / marry ?
4 divorce / Why / Bruno / she / did ?
5 for / Did / Andy Dixon / play / Liverpool ?
6 did / How / Walden United / score / many / goals ?

b) 🔟47 In pairs. Answer the example questions a) and b) and questions (1–6) in Exercise 5a). Then listen to the news stories again and check.

6 a) Look at Recording script 47 on page 139. Then write five false sentences.

Example: Andy Dixon scored six goals.

b) Go round the class and say your sentences. The other students must correct them.

Example: A: Andy Dixon scored six goals.
B: No, he didn't. He scored two goals.

Pronunciation: /d/, /t/ or /ɪd/

7 a) 🔟48 We can pronounce the -(e)d ending of regular verbs in the Past Simple in three ways: /d/, /t/, or /ɪd/. Listen and fill in the table below with the verbs from the Word Box.

destroyed ✓ jumped ✓ arrested ✓ escaped
arrived played started phoned married
invited divorced injured surprised

/d/	/t/	/ɪd/
destroyed	jumped	arrested
....	....	....
....	....	....
....	....	....
....	....	....
....	....	....
....	....	....
....	....	....

b) 🔟49 Listen and check. Then listen again and repeat.

Shopper sees Elvis in local store

When Mrs Dolly Cline went to her local supermarket last Saturday she had the surprise of her life! She saw her favourite singer, Elvis Presley, next to the ice-cream freezer. Dolly spoke to Elvis but he didn't speak to her. She took a photograph of the star and he gave her his autograph. Then he bought a bottle of diet cola and left.

Past Simple of irregular verbs

8 **a)** Read this newspaper article. Dolly Cline had a big surprise last weekend. What happened?

b) Answer these questions about the article.

1 Where did Dolly see Elvis?
2 What did Elvis do?
3 What did he buy?

9 Read the article again and underline the eight positive Past Simple verbs. Then fill in the gaps in the Language Box below.

Past Simple of irregular verbs

Verb	Past Simple	Verb	Past Simple
....	bought	....	saw
....	gave	....	spoke
....	had	....	took
....	left	go	went

Negative sentences
We use *didn't* + verb to make negative sentences – the same as regular verbs.
Elvis **didn't speak** to her.

Questions
We use *did* + verb to make questions – the same as regular verbs.
Did Dolly **see** Elvis?

10 **a)** A journalist from the local newspaper is interviewing Dolly. Fill in the gaps with *did* or *didn't*.

JOURNALIST: I didn't see Elvis. .... you see him?
DOLLY: Yes, I ....
JOURNALIST: .... he speak to you?
DOLLY: No, he ....
JOURNALIST: Where .... you see him?
DOLLY: Next to the ice-cream freezer.

b) ●●50 There are four mistakes about Dolly in the newspaper article. Listen to this radio news report and find the mistakes in the article. Then listen again and correct them.

6

Time expressions for the past

11 Look at the Language Box on the right. Then fill in the gaps with *last* or *ago*.

Example: Andy divorced his wife a month ago.

1 Where did you go .... night?
2 Did you see Claudia .... week?
3 I bought a new car three weeks ....
4 .... July they went to Australia.
5 We didn't have a holiday .... year.
6 Mr Presley isn't here. He left ten minutes ....

When did you last . . . ?

12 a) Fill in the questionnaire for yourself. Then write two more questions with verbs from this unit.

b) Go round the class and ask two students the questions. Fill in the questionnaire for them. Ask more questions.

Example: A: When did you last see a film?
　　　　　 B: Last week. OR A week ago.
　　　　　 A: What did you see?
　　　　　 B: I saw . . .

When did you last . . . ?

		Me	Student A	Student B
1	see a film?	....	....	....
2	go to a nice restaurant?	....	....	....
3	take a taxi?	....	....	....
4	buy a book?	....	....	....
5	give someone a present?	....	....	....
6	phone a friend?	....	....	....
7	invite a friend to your house?	....	....	....
8	have a holiday?	....	....	....
9	.... ?	....	....	....
10	.... ?	....	....	....

Conversations *Oh, really?*

1 **a)** 🎧51 Look at the photograph of the party at Jean's flat. Listen to the conversation. How do Hannah and Nick know Jean?

b) 🎧51 Fill in the gaps with the words from the Word Box. Then listen and check.

> really (x 2)　　　sorry　　　right

HANNAH: Hi, Jean.
JEAN: Hi, Hannah. How are you?
HANNAH: I'm OK. What about you?
JEAN: Fine, thanks. Um, Hannah, do you know Nick?
HANNAH: No, I don't.
JEAN: Well, Hannah, this is Nick. And Nick, this is Hannah.
NICK: Hi, Hannah.
HANNAH: Hi. Nice to meet you.
JEAN: Excuse me, there's the door. Back in a minute.
NICK: OK. See you. So, uh, how do you know Jean?
HANNAH: Oh, I'm her neighbour.
NICK: Oh, ...
HANNAH: What about you?
NICK: .... ?
HANNAH: What about you? How do you know Jean?
NICK: Oh, I work with her.
HANNAH: Oh, ... ? So, do you work in the Sales Department, too?
NICK: No. I'm a designer.
HANNAH: Oh, ... ?

2 **a)** Which of the words in the Word Box in Exercise 1b) do Hannah, Nick and Jean use to:

1 show interest and that they are listening?
2 ask someone to repeat?

b) 🎧52 Listen. Do the words go up ↗ or down ↘ at the end? Write ↗ or ↘ in the boxes. Then listen again and repeat the reactions.

1 Oh, really? ☐　　　3 Sorry? ☐
2 Really? ☐　　　4 Right. ☐

3 Find these words in the conversation. Why do the speakers use them?

> um　　　well　　　so　　　uh　　　oh

4 🎧53 Listen and react after each person speaks. Show interest or ask them to repeat.

5 In groups of three. Have conversations like the one in Exercise 1b) but change the information in blue.

6 **a)** 🎧54 Listen. Which question is Hannah answering?

1 What do you do on holiday?
2 What's your favourite place? Why?

b) 🎧54 Listen again. What does Hannah say about her sister's house?

c) Think about the questions in Exercise 6a). What are your answers? Write some key words.

d) In groups of three. Ask and answer the questions in Exercise 6a).

Reading for pleasure

③ The red dress

1 Before you read the story, look at the title and the picture. What do you think the story is about?

2 🔊 55 Read and listen to the first part of the story. Then fill in the gaps in the paragraph below.

> Here I am, in my new flat. In a new city. In a new life. Tomorrow I start a new job. I'd like a new name and a new face but it isn't possible.
>
> This is a lovely flat. The twenty-second floor. From the windows I can see the city. It's dark now but the sky is full of light. There are thousands of lights shining brightly in the city. They're like jewels – white diamonds, red rubies, green emeralds.

The story is about a young woman. She has a new .... in a different city. Tomorrow is her first day in a new .... The flat has a view of the ....

3 🔊 56 Read and listen to the next part of the story. Then fill in the gaps in the paragraph below.

> In the bedroom, I open my suitcase and take out my clothes. Grey skirts, grey jackets, black trousers, black sweaters. I don't like people to look at me.

All her clothes are .... or .... because she doesn't want people to .... her.

4 Read the two parts again. Are these sentences true (T) or false (F)? Correct the false sentences.

Example: This young woman is trying to
forget her past. ⬛T
It's day time. ⬛F
It isn't day time. It's night time.

1 She is spending her last night in her old flat. ☐
2 The flat is in a tall building. ☐
3 She doesn't like the lights in the city. ☐
4 She likes red, yellow and blue clothes. ☐

5 Now read the whole story. It starts on page 9 of *On the same wavelength and other stories.* What happens next? Think about these questions while you read:

1 What does the young woman find in the wardrobe?
2 What does she find in a drawer?
3 Who put them there?
4 How old is the young woman?
5 Is her life interesting?
6 Why are the weekends long for her?
7 Why does the telephone never ring?
8 Who do you think is in the other half of the cut photograph?
9 What does the young woman dream about?
10 What does the young woman do when she doesn't go to work?
11 What does she do at the end of the story?
12 Who is the man in the lift?

Round the world

Past Simple of irregular verbs
Past Simple of *be: was / were*
Skills: Murder at Hadley Hall!

Past Simple of irregular verbs

1 a) Liz went on a trip round the world. She sent some photographs and a letter to her friend, Anna. Look at the photographs. Which four countries do you think she went to?

b) Read these parts of Liz's letter (1–4) and match them to the photographs (a–d).

Example: 1 = d)

Dear Anna,

Well, I'm finally writing! I'm sorry this letter is so late. I had an amazing trip.

1

It was beautiful there but the weather wasn't good – in fact it was awful. It was hot and wet – and there were mosquitoes everywhere. I felt ill for a week. Then we met some local people on a boat. They didn't speak English, but they understood I was ill and they gave me some medicine. It helped a lot. When I felt OK again I went to . . .

2

I was there in December and it was very beautiful. I spent three days in the mountains. The people were nice, but very shy. I had a really good guide. He was very friendly. He knew the area well and spoke good English. After that I went to . . .

3

I spent a week there in February and had a really good time. The weather was fantastic and I thought the beaches were amazing. The sea was beautiful – really clear and blue. I slept and swam a lot. I ate fresh fish and tropical fruit every day – and I drank delicious cocktails in the evening. I also heard some great music and bought some lovely jewellery. When I left I was really sad because my trip was almost finished. The last place I went to was . . .

4

I hated it because it was really noisy and the people weren't very friendly. On the first day I lost my passport and someone stole my watch. Luckily the waitress in the hotel restaurant found my passport in the ladies' toilet! I didn't find my watch, of course. It wasn't a good end to my trip . . .

2 Read Liz's letter again and underline the positive Past Simple verbs (not *was*, *were*). Then fill in the gaps in the Language Box on the right. Check your answers in the Irregular verb list on page 143.

3 a) Make negative sentences.

Example: Local people gave Liz medicine. They <u>didn't give</u> her food.

1 Liz's guide spoke English. He .... French.
2 Liz ate fish and tropical fruit. She .... meat.
3 Liz drank cocktails in the evening. She .... beer.
4 Liz found her passport. She .... her watch.

b) 🔊 57 Listen and check.

4 a) When Liz got home, her sister, Jade, phoned her and asked a lot of questions. Write Jade's questions and Liz's answers in the Past Simple.

Examples: Who / meet?

JADE: Who did you meet?   LIZ: I <u>met</u> some local people.

they / speak English?

JADE: Did they speak English?   LIZ: No, they <u>didn't</u>.

Jade's questions	Liz's answers
1 What / give you?	They .... me some medicine.
2 How many days / spend in the mountains?	I .... three days there.
3 your guide / speak English?	Yes, he .... He .... good English.
4 swim / a lot in February?	Yes, I .... I .... every day.
5 What / eat?	I .... fish and fruit.
6 What / drink?	I .... delicious cocktails.
7 lose / your passport?	Yes, I ....
8 find / your watch?	No, I ....

b) 🔊 58 Listen and check.

5 Do you like travelling? In pairs. Choose four countries to visit and talk about your reasons.

Example: I'd like to go to <u>the USA</u> because I really want to <u>go to Disneyland</u>.

Past Simple of irregular verbs

Verb	Past Simple
buy	<u>bought</u>
drink	....
eat	....
feel	....
find	....
give	....
go	....
have	....
hear	....
know	....
leave	....
lose	....
meet	....
sleep	....
speak	....
spend	....
steal	....
swim	....
think	....
understand	....

Past Simple of *be: was / were*

6 Read Liz's letter on page 47 again and underline *was*, *wasn't*, *were*, *weren't*. Then fill in the gaps in the Language Box on the right.

7 In groups of three. Correct these sentences. Use the pictures to help you.

Example: A: Cleopatra was the queen of England.
B: No, she wasn't the queen of England.
C: She was the queen of Egypt.

1 Romeo and Juliet were American.
2 The mini skirt was famous in the 1860s.
3 Picasso and Van Gogh were famous politicians.
4 John F Kennedy was a pop singer.
5 Marilyn Monroe was an English teacher.

Past Simple of *be*

Present

	Positive	Negative
I	'm	
you		
we		
they		
he		
she		
it		

Past

	Positive	Negative
I		
you		
we		
they		
he		
she		
it		wasn't

8 **a)** Look at the picture. Why do you think John is angry with Maria? Read their conversation and find out. Then fill in the gaps with *was, wasn't, were* or *weren't*. What do you think happened next?

MARIA: What's wrong, darling?
JOHN: Where ..*were*.... you yesterday afternoon?
MARIA: I .... at the office.
JOHN: No, you .... I phoned the office at three o' clock. You .... there. .... you with him?
MARIA: No, I ....
JOHN: Yes, you .... ! I know it!
MARIA: Oh, don't be stupid!
JOHN: .... he in Paris with you last week?
MARIA: No, he .... I .... alone!

b) 🔊59 Listen and check. Then fill in the gaps in the Language Box on the right with *was, wasn't, were* or *weren't*.

Pronunciation: *was / were*

9 **a)** 🔊60 Read and listen to these sentences. Are *was, wasn't, were* and *weren't* stressed or weak? Fill in the boxes with S (stressed) or W (weak). When do we stress these words and when are they weak?

SENTENCES AND QUESTIONS

1 /wəz/ a) I was ☐ at the office.
b) Was ☐ he in Paris?

2 /wə/ a) You were ☐ with him.
b) Where were ☐ you yesterday?

NEGATIVES AND SHORT ANSWERS

3 /wɒzənt/ a) He wasn't ☐ in Paris.
b) No, I wasn't ☐.

4 /wɒz/ a) Yes, I was ☐.
b) Yes, he was ☐.

5 /wɜːnt/ a) You weren't ☐ there.
b) No, you weren't ☐.

6 /wɜː/ a) Yes, you were ☐.
b) Yes, we were ☐.

b) 🔊60 Listen again and repeat. In pairs, read the conversation from Exercise 8a).

Where did you go?

10 In groups of four. Student A, look at page 116; Student B at page 118; Student C at page 121; and Student D at page 122.

Past Simple of *be*: questions and short answers

Yes / No questions
A: .... I / he / she / it in Paris last week?
A: .... you / we / they in Paris last week?

Positive answers
B: Yes, I / he / she / it ....
B: Yes, you / we / they ....

Negative answers
C: No, I / he / she / it ....
C: No, you / we / they ....

Grammar reference and puzzles
Past Simple of regular and irregular verbs: pages 106–107

Skills *Reading, speaking*

1 Read the headline and look at the picture below. Then answer the questions.

1 What happened at Hadley Hall?

2 Look at the triangle. Then find Lord Pimm, Lady Pimm, the maid, the butler, the cook and the gardener in the picture.

Lord Cedric Pimm   Lady Matilda Pimm

?

Tom Wiggit, the butler

Jenny Wiggit, the cook

Freddie Kettle, the gardener

Ruth Kettle, the maid

Murder at Hadley Hall!
Who shot the gardener?

Sunday
Why did I marry Ruth? She's a fool. She was rude to Lady Pimm today. They had an argument about money. Ruth wants more money, but Lady Pimm said "No!".

Monday
I saw Lady Pimm today. She was angry with Ruth. She wanted her to leave Hadley Hall. I talked to her for a long time. She's OK now. Ruth can stay here.

Tuesday
Lord Pimm's a fool. He gave his wife another diamond last week. She gave it to me today! Ha!

Wednesday
Lady Pimm saw me with Jenny today in the garden. Beautiful Jenny! Why does she love that fool, Tom?

Thursday
Lady Pimm came to the garden this morning – she's jealous of Jenny and she wanted to talk to me. She's OK now I think – but old Pimm saw her with me and he was really angry this afternoon. I know he's jealous of me.

Friday
My darling Jenny was sad today. Why did she marry that fool Tom?! I saw him with Ruth again. What's happening?

Saturday
I talked to Tom about my money again. He still can't give it back to me! He was really angry. He's so stupid!

Wavelength page

2 a) In groups of three. Read the gardener's diary and talk about the information. Who were the people at Hadley Hall married to? Who did they love / hate? Why?

b) Start to fill in the Motives table on page 128.

c) Work together to find out who murdered the gardener. Student A, look at page 116; Student B at page 118 and Student C at page 120.

3 In your group. Answer these questions.

1 Who visited Hadley Hall before the murder?
2 What did John Woodson see in the garden?
3 What did Freddie want from Tom?
4 Why did Jenny and Tom have money problems?
5 Was Freddie a good husband to Ruth?
6 Why was Lord Pimm worried about his and Lady Pimm's bank account?
7 What did Lady Pimm buy at the jeweller's?
8 Why was Lord Pimm angry on the evening of the murder?
9 Who was the murderer? Who shot Freddie Kettle?

8 Trains and boats and planes

Types of transport and travel verbs
Past Simple: travel verbs
I'm sorry I'm late
Do you remember? Units 5–8

Types of transport and travel verbs

1 What type of transport do you think the people are using? Match the words in the Word Box to the pictures (a–i).

> bike / bicycle /baɪsɪkəl/   bus   car   motorbike
> plane   the Underground / the Tube   boat   train   taxi

2 Match the sentences with the same meaning.

Example: 1 = d)

1 I went by bus / train.   a) I drove.
2 I went by plane.   b) I walked.
3 I went by car.   c) I cycled.
4 I went on foot.   d) I took the bus / train.
5 I rode my bike.   e) I flew.

3 Fill in the gaps with the correct prepositions from the Word Box.

> on   into   out of   off

1 You get .... and .... a car or taxi.
2 You get .... and .... a bike / bicycle, boat, bus, plane, motorbike, train or the Underground / the Tube.

Travel questionnaire

	Name	When?	Where?	How much?	How long?
1 Take a bus?					
2 Take a taxi?					
3 Fly somewhere?					
4 Drive a car?					
5 Ride a bike?					
6 Ride a motorbike?					
7 Take the train?					

4 a) Look at the questionnaire. Then write these words in the correct order and make four questions about 1 (Take a bus?).

1 you / take / When / bus / did / last / a ?
2 go / you / Where / did ?
3 it / much / How / cost / did ?
4 take / it / did / long / How ?

b) Make similar questions for (2–7).

c) Then go round the class. Take it in turns to ask and answer questions and fill in the questionnaire.

5 Look at the picture of Phil and Linda and the Language Box below. Then fill in the gaps with the correct form of *come* or *go*.

Example: I came to your office but you weren't there.

1 .... here, Mary. I need to speak to you.
2 We're having a party on Saturday. Can you .... ?
3 I .... to India last Christmas. It was great.
4 Carol's not here, Adam. She .... home early.
5 I always .... to my friend's house by bus.

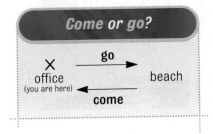

Come or go?

Why didn't you **come** to the office yesterday?

I **went** to the beach but don't tell anyone.

Past Simple: travel verbs

6 **a)** Look at the pictures and read the story about James. Then fill in the gaps with the Past Simple of the verbs in the Word Box.

> arrive buy drive get into get off (x 2) get on (x 4)
> leave get out of fly take walk (x 2)

b) 🔊 61 Listen and check.

c) In pairs. Where did the man go? What do you think was in James's briefcase? What do you think happened next?

① James .... his car and smoked a cigarette. He wanted to run away but he knew there was no escape.

② He .... to the station.

③ At the station he .... the car and looked slowly round.

④ He took a small, black briefcase from the back seat and .... into the station.

⑤ He .... a ticket and waited on the platform.

⑥ When the train ...., he .... and sat down next to a woman reading a foreign newspaper.

⑦ At the next station the woman .... with the briefcase.

⑧ She .... quickly to a bus stop.

⑨ She sat down on a bench. A bus came but she didn't .... A large man with a beard .... the bus. He sat down next to the woman. They didn't speak.

⑩ The woman .... the next bus without the briefcase.

⑪ The man then picked up the briefcase and ....

⑫ He .... a taxi to the airport.

⑬ THIS IS THE LAST CALL FOR FLIGHT BA1253 TO . . .

He waited in the bar. Then at 9:30 p.m. he .... a plane and .... to . . .

I'm sorry I'm late

7 **a)** Look at these excuses. Four of them are not reasons to be late. Which four?

1 I missed the bus.
2 I got up early.
3 My car broke down.
4 The traffic was terrible.
5 The train was on time.

6 The train was late.
7 I took a taxi.
8 I took the wrong bus.
9 There was an accident.
10 There wasn't any traffic.

b) Now match the six reasons to be late in Exercise 7a) to the information (a–e) to show the meaning.

Example: I ran to the bus stop, but the bus left before I got there. I shouted and waved my arms but it didn't stop. ☐1

a) There were a lot of cars and buses on the streets this morning. It was awful! ☐

b) I was in Regent Street and suddenly my car stopped. I pushed it to the garage. ☐

c) I forgot my glasses this morning. I got on the 253, not the 263. ☐

d) A car crashed into a bus. Luckily no one was hurt. ☐

e) The timetable said 9:30, but the train didn't leave until 9:50! ☐

8 **a)** 🔊62 Look at the photograph. Nina is late for work. She's apologising to her boss, Mr Green. Listen and answer the questions.

1 Do you think this is the first time she is late?
2 Is Mr Green angry with Nina?

b) 🔊62 Listen again. Which four excuses from Exercise 7a) does Nina use?

Excuses, excuses

9 In pairs. Choose two of these pairs and have conversations like Nina's. Take it in turns to apologise and react. Use the notes on page 123 to help you.

1 boss and employee
2 parent and child
3 husband and wife
4 girlfriend and boyfriend

Sorry I'm late, Mr Green, but . . .

1 Talking about places

a) What is Dave asking Phil? Make his questions.

b) In pairs. Now have a similar conversation about a place you visited.

I went to Brazil.

Where / go?

How much / cost?

go with friends?

How long / stay there?

What / see?

2 *Where were you?*

a) 👀 63 Read the article on the right. Then listen. It's Tuesday evening. A police officer is interviewing a young woman about the crime. Listen and match the times *(When?)* to the places *(Where?)*.

When?
1 Last Wednesday.
2 On Thursday.
3 At six o'clock on Friday.
4 At the weekend.
5 Yesterday morning.
6 Last night.
7 An hour ago.

Where?
a) I wasn't at work. I was ill.
b) I was in my car. The traffic was terrible.
c) I was in a café.
d) I was at the university.
e) I was at a friend's house.
f) I was at the office.
g) I was at home with my family.

b) Go round the class. Ask and answer questions about the times in Exercise 2a).

Example: A: Where were you last Wednesday?
B: Well, I was here in the college with you and in the evening . . .

3 *He looks fantastic!*

Make a list of all the words for clothes you know. Then, in groups of four, compare your lists. Use your ideas and finish these sentences.

Example: He looks fantastic! He's wearing a pink suit and a green tie!

1 She looks lovely. She's . . . .
2 He looks awful. He's . . . .
3 She looks boring. She's . . . .
4 He looks interesting. He's . . . .

4 The hotel receptionist game

Look at the picture on the right. The guest has a bad cold and can't speak. In groups of three. Take it in turns to be the guest and the two receptionists. Student A, look at page 117; Student B at page 119; and Student C at page 121.

Look at the Word lists for Units 5–8 on pages 133–135 and check that you know all the new words.

Love-sick student smashed professor's windows

Psychology professor Theo Silk arrived home last night after a holiday in France. While he was away someone broke all the windows in his house. The police are looking for a female student who wrote Professor Silk some letters.

Do you . . . ?

Would you like a . . . ?

I'd like a taxi to the airport.

Did you . . . ?

Reception

Is your room . . . ?

Are you . . . ?

Wavelength page

Reading for pleasure

④ Rats

1 What do you think makes a perfect married couple? Read these sentences and tick the ones you agree with.

It's important that husbands and wives:
1 have the same interests.
2 work in the same area.
3 are both successful in their jobs.
4 have a lot of money.
5 are good-looking.
6 have children.
7 live in a nice place.
8 are in love.

2 Before you read the story, look at the title and the pictures. What do you think the story is about?

3 🎧 64 Read and listen to the first part of the story on the right. Then answer the questions.

1 Were Marsha and Justin "the perfect married couple"?
2 What did Marsha do?
3 What did Justin do?
4 Where did they live?

4 🎧 65 Read and listen to the next part of the story and look at the pictures on the right. Then answer the questions.

1 What were Marsha and Justin's two serious problems?
2 Which problem did they never talk about?
3 Why do you think they had the first problem?

5 Now read the whole story. It starts on page 12 of *On the same wavelength and other stories*. What happened next? Did Marsha and Justin kill the rats? Think about these questions while you read.

1 What time of year was it? Which month?
2 What did Marsha buy for the rats?
3 What did Marsha do when she got home?
4 What made her angry?
5 What did she do next?
6 Why did she have a hot bath?
7 What else did she find and put in the bathroom?
8 Why didn't she hear Justin come home?
9 What made Justin angry?
10 What did he do when he went upstairs to the bathroom?
11 What did he do after that?

Marsha and Justin Hammond were the perfect married couple. They were young and good-looking, they had money, they were successful in their jobs. She worked in advertising, he worked in television. They lived in an old but fashionable part of town. The buildings were once small factories – now they were smart, expensive houses.

But the Hammonds had two very serious problems. They often talked about one of the problems . . .

We must do something about those rats!

SQUEAK!

SQUEAK!

SQUEAK!

OK, OK, I'll buy something tomorrow.

. . . but they never talked about the other problem.

You're so boring.

I don't love you any more.

Media News

9

He has personality and looks

Adjectives for people: *What's he like? He's shy.*
What does she look like? She's tall.
Conversations: *Oh, no!*

Adjectives for people

1 a) Look at the pictures. They show scenes from a new Hollywood film *Rick Channing – Private Detective*. Read the list of parts and the filmscripts. Then match the pictures of the scenes (1–5) to the filmscripts (a–e). Fill in the numbers.

b) 🔊 66 Listen and check.

PARTS			
Rick Channing	private detective	**Chantalle Duvalier**	his first daughter
Eugene Duvalier III	a rich businessman	**Violet Duvalier**	his second daughter
Loretta Duvalier	his second wife	**Randolf Duvalier**	his second son

ⓐ

SCENE ☐1

Eugene Duvalier III phones Rick Channing. He has a problem. His first son, Eugene Duvalier IV, is missing.

CHANNING: So, what's the problem, Mr Duvalier?
DUVALIER: He has some bad friends. He's never at home. He's rude to his stepmother and he's very strange sometimes.
CHANNING: So, what's new?
DUVALIER: Stop joking, Channing. We don't know where he is. I want you to find him. Do you want the job?
CHANNING: I want the money.
DUVALIER: Right. Come to my house tonight at seven o'clock.

ⓑ

SCENE ☐

CHANNING: Hello. I'm Rick Channing.
VIOLET: Oh, hello. I'm Violet. Nice to meet you, Mr Channing.
RANDOLF: He's here about Eugene IV.
VIOLET: Oh, I see. Poor Eugene.
RANDOLF: Yes, well. My sister studies music, Mr Channing.
CHANNING: I see. A musician in the family.
VIOLET: Oh, but I'm not very good.
RANDOLF: Don't be silly. You're fantastic.
VIOLET: Mr Channing, would you like some iced tea?
CHANNING: Sure. Thank you.

What are you doing for the rest of your life?

The future: Present Continuous
The future: 'll (will) + verb
Day to day English: Arrangements

The future: Present Continuous

1 **a)** Are you organised? Read the questionnaire. Then write one more question.

b) In pairs. Take it in turns to ask and answer the questions and fill in the questionnaire. Who is more organised?

2 ⚏ 71 Look at the photograph. It's Friday evening. Susan and Mark work together. They're talking about the weekend. Read this list. Then listen and tick (✓) the eight things they talk about.

1 a drink with Dave ☐
2 golf ☐
3 a driving lesson ☐
4 tennis ☐
5 a dinner party ☐
6 Roger's parents ☐
7 a concert ☐
8 a birthday party ☐
9 New York ☐
10 a film ☐

Are you **organised?**

	You	Your partner
1 Do you wear a watch?		
2 Are you very late for appointments?		
3 Do you use an alarm clock every morning?		
4 Do you use a diary or calendar to arrange your social life?		
5 What would you like to do this weekend? Have you got any arrangements?		
6 .... ?		

3 a) 71 Look at Susan's diary. Listen again. Use the information from Exercise 2 and fill it in.

	Friday	Saturday	Sunday
morning	work	....	....
afternoon	work	....	....
evening	a drink with Dave	....	....

b) 72 Listen to the first part of the conversation again. Fill in the gaps in Mark's question and Susan's answer. Then answer the questions.

So, ... this weekend?
Well, I'm very busy. Tonight .... with Dave.

1 Are Susan and Mark using the Present Continuous or the Present Simple?
2 Are they talking about the present or the future?
3 Do you think Susan arranges her social life?
4 Do you think Mark arranges his social life?

4 a) Sally is a friend of Susan's. Last night Sally left a message on Susan's answerphone. This morning Susan left Sally a message. What did Susan say? Use her diary in Exercise 3a) and the verbs in the Word Box.

BT
PLAY
Susan, this is Sally. Can we meet this weekend? What are you doing?

see	drive	have (x 2)	play	go (x 2)

Example: Sally, it's Susan. I'm sorry, I can't see you this weekend. I'm really busy. Tonight I'm . . .

b) Look at Recording script 71 on page 140 and check your answers.

1
Dear ....,
What about dinner in Paris tonight?
Love, Felix
a
Dear ....,
Sorry, I'm playing golf in Miami on Tuesday. What about Wednesday?
Marc
2
Dear ....,
Would you like to fly to St Tropez on Tuesday and go swimming?
Masako

5 **a)** Look at the international jet-setters. Match the invitations (1–3) to the answers (a–c). Fill in the names.

b) You're a busy international jet-setter. Make a diary for next week. Think about what you would like to do. Write an e-mail to a student in the class and invite him / her to do something with you. Send your invitation.

c) Write a reply to the invitation you get, saying *Yes* (*Yes, that sounds nice / great.*) or *No* (*Sorry, I'm . . .*). If you say *No*, suggest another day (*What about Tuesday?*). Continue inviting and replying until your diary is full.

d) In groups of four. Compare your diaries. Which diary is the most interesting?

Dear ....,
Sorry, I'm busy tonight.
I'm going to a film
première in London.
Mirka

Dear ....,
Yeah, I'm free on Friday.
That sounds great.
Pedro

Dear ....,
How about a party at
MGM studios in
Hollywood on Friday?
Helena

The future: 'll (will) + verb

6 🔊 73 Look at the photograph. Listen and read the conversation. Then answer the questions.

SAM: What are you doing tonight, Mark?

MARK: Oh, er, I don't know. Maybe I'll see a film or go to the pub. I'm not sure.

SAM: Are you going to Paul's party tomorrow?

MARK: Oh, I'm not sure. Perhaps I will. Are you going?

1 Does Mark have definite arrangements for tonight and tomorrow?

2 What does he say to show that he isn't sure about his weekend?

3 What does Mark say after *maybe* and *perhaps*?

7 a) Fill in the gaps in the Language Box on the right with the Present Continuous or *maybe / perhaps* + *'ll (will)* + verb.

b) Write sentences and questions with the Present Continuous or *'ll (will)* + verb.

Example: (meet) I'm meeting my bank manager tomorrow morning.

1 (you / do) A: What .... on Saturday?
  (go) B: I don't know. There's a party at Paul's. Maybe I......................... .

2 (come) A: Dave...................... to the pub tonight. He told me yesterday.
  (not / come) B: Oh. I don't like him very much. Perhaps I ....

3 (you / fly) A: .... to France?
  (take) B: I'm not sure. It's expensive. Perhaps I......................... the train.

4 (not / see) A: Maybe I......................... Sam tonight. I have a lot of work.

Are you busy?

8 a) What are you really doing this week? Write three ideas and three definite arrangements. Use the time expressions in the Word Box.

> at the weekend   on Tuesday / Friday   tomorrow evening
> this evening   tonight   on Saturday morning

Example: Maybe I'll go to the beach at the weekend. (idea)
On Friday I'm meeting a friend. (arrangement)

b) Go round the class and have conversations with the other students.

Example: A: What are you doing at the weekend?
B: I don't know. Maybe I'll go to the country. What about you?

> **Present Continuous OR maybe / perhaps + 'll (will) + verb**
>
> We use ....
> when we talk about our **definite** future arrangements.
> When we talk about our **ideas** for the future (not our definite arrangements) we can use ....
> ....
>
> **Positive sentences**
> I'm **going** to the cinema tomorrow.
> Maybe / perhaps **I'll (I will) go** to the cinema.
>
> **Negative sentences**
> I'm **not playing** tennis tomorrow.
> Maybe / perhaps **I won't (I will not) play** tennis.

> *Grammar reference and puzzles*
>
> The future: Present Continuous and *'ll (will)* + verb: page 108

Day to day English *Arrangements*

Saying *Yes* and *No* to invitations

1 **a)** In pairs. Look at the picture. Do you think Linda wants to go out with Phil? What do you think they are saying? Fill in the gaps.

PHIL: Hi, Linda. How's it going?
LINDA: OK.
PHIL: Uh, Linda? .... a film on Friday?
LINDA: Oh, sorry, Phil. .... a party on Friday.
PHIL: Oh, never mind. Maybe another time, eh?

b) 🔊 74 Listen and check. Then, in pairs, practise the conversation.

2 **a)** Now Dave is talking to Linda. Read their conversation and answer the questions below.

DAVE: Hey, Linda, would you like to see a film tonight?
LINDA: Yeah, that sounds nice. What shall we see?
DAVE: I don't mind.
LINDA: What about seeing the new Tarantino film?
DAVE: OK. Where's it on?
LINDA: The Odeon.
DAVE: Yeah, OK. What time shall we meet?
LINDA: It's up to you. It starts at 7:15.
DAVE: How about seven, then?
LINDA: Yes. Seven's fine. Shall we meet at the cinema?
DAVE: All right. Let's have dinner after the film.
LINDA: Good idea. See you at seven.
DAVE: Right. See you at the cinema at seven then. Bye.

1 Did Linda tell Phil the truth about the party?
2 Does she want to go out with Dave?
3 What are they doing this evening?
4 Where are they meeting and when?

b) Read the conversation again and answer these questions.

1 Which words do Linda and Dave use to ask for and make suggestions?
2 Which words do they use to say *Yes* to invitations and suggestions?
3 Linda says something which means *I don't mind*. What does she say?

c) 🔊 75 Listen and repeat the suggestions. Then in pairs practise the conversation.

3 **a)** A friend is coming to your town / city for the weekend. It's his / her first visit. Make a list of four places to go to. Think why the places are good.

b) In pairs. Take it in turns to be the visitor. Plan your weekend together.

Wavelength page

Reading for pleasure

⑤ On the same wavelength

On the same
Wavelength
and other stories

LONGMAN — Elaine O'Reilly

1 Before you read the story, look at the title. What do you think it means?

1 To communicate through radio or other kinds of technology.
2 To understand someone because you speak the same language.
3 To understand someone because you both have the same opinions and feelings.

2 🔊 76 Read and listen to a), the first part of the story. Then answer the questions.

1 Where was Mark?
2 What changed each time Mark tried to send the message?
3 Who did he want to communicate with?
4 Why were communications down?
5 How much oxygen was there?

3 🔊 77 Read and listen to b), a later part of the story. Then answer the questions.

1 What was the crisis in 2050?
2 Who solved the problem?
3 What was the solution?
4 What kind of children did they produce?

4 Before you read the whole story try to answer these questions.

1 Mark had a number (18) instead of a surname. Why do you think that was?
2 What do you think happened to Mark?
   a) He killed the virus in the oxygen supply.
   b) He was saved before the oxygen ran out.
   c) He died but he had a clone on Earth.

5 Now read the whole story. It starts on page 16 of *On the same wavelength and other stories*. Think about these questions while you read.

1 How many brothers did Mark have?
2 When were they all born?
3 What was Mark's nickname? Why?
4 Was his job on Space Station KCQ 371 difficult? Why / Why not?
5 Was he lonely on the space station? Why / Why not?
6 What did Mark hear when he was on the platform outside the space station?
7 What was their message?
8 How did his brothers know about his problem?
9 Who did Mark talk to in the space station?

ⓐ

The big computer bleeped.
"Let's try again," thought Mark.

He touched the repeat key. Again his message came up on the monitor. The same message for twelve days now. Only the date was different each time.

> **20 June 2076**
> **To**   Houston Base
> **From Mark 18**
>   Space Station KCQ 371
>
> SOS
> ALL COMMUNICATIONS ARE
> DOWN – UNKNOWN VIRUS
> IN THE OXYGEN SYSTEM.
> OXYGEN ENDS 27 JUNE.
> DATA FOLLOWING.

Mark clicked on the data icon and information came up on the monitor – lists of statistics on the space station's facilities. There was enough food and water for three more months but there was only enough oxygen for one more week. The virus meant time was running out for Mark 18 – fast.

ⓑ

Around 2050 there was a world population crisis – there were not enough young people. At the same time scientists perfected human cloning, so suddenly there was a solution to the problem. In laboratories all over the world, scientists cloned thousands of children. And all of them were clever and strong and good-looking.

Skills *Listening, reading, writing*

11

Skills *Listening, reading, writing*

1 a) Match the words from the Word Box to the things in the photograph.

> knife   fork   spoon   plate   toast
> mug   bacon   fried eggs   sausages /sɒsɪdʒɪz/
> milk   sugar   butter   marmalade   cereal

b) 🔊 80 Listen. What do these two British people have for breakfast?

2 a) Read the article below quickly. Which restaurant was good?

b) Read the article again. Underline the adjectives. Make notes about the two restaurants.

3 a) 🔊 81 Listen. Match Charles and Edwina's conversations to the restaurants.

1 ....   2 ....

b) 🔊 82 Listen to the beginning of Conversation 2 again. Fill in the gaps in the questions.

1 .... sausages ....?
2 .... mushrooms?
3 .... eggs?

4 In pairs. You're having a meal (breakfast, lunch or dinner) in a restaurant. Is it good or bad? Write a conversation about the food, drink and service.

Examples: A: What's the bread like?
                 B: It's delicious, really fresh.

The Great British Breakfast?

by Edwina Harris and Charles Mortimer

How good is the Great British Breakfast? We sent two of our best journalists, Charles Mortimer and Edwina Harris, to restaurants around the country to find out.

The Royal, The Strand, London W1

Congratulations to the chef! This is a beautiful English restaurant in the heart of London and it serves the perfect English breakfast. The orange juice is fresh and delicious. There are tasty beef and pork sausages. We especially liked the mushrooms – they arrive fresh from Scotland every day – and are fantastic. It's expensive of course!

The Tempest, Bridge Street, Stratford-upon-Avon

There are too many restaurants like this! It's a nice little place with pretty pink tablecloths, but these were the only good things. The service was very slow. Our waiter was polite, when he finally arrived, but we waited half an hour for our meal! The bacon was greasy and the sausages were tasteless. The bread was definitely not fresh and we asked for fresh orange juice but they gave us juice from a carton! The meal cost £30 for two and was definitely not value for money! We don't recommend this restaurant to anyone who loves good food.

Wavelength page

It's bigger and better

Comparing: comparative adjectives;
   not as + adjective + *as*
Prepositions of place: *Where's . . . ?*
Do you remember? Units 9–12

Comparing

Comparative adjectives

1 a) ⊙⊙ 83 Look at the picture. Fred is on holiday with his wife, Wilma. Terry and Debbie are on their honeymoon. What are the two couples like? Listen and find out. Then answer the questions.

1 Tick (✓) the things they talk about.
   a) the weather ☐   d) the hotels ☐
   b) the food ☐   e) the buses ☐
   c) the shops ☐   f) the beaches ☐
2 Where are the people on holiday?
3 Which couple is staying at the Plaza Hotel?
4 Which couple is staying at the Grand Hotel?

b) [oo] 83 Look at the pictures on the right. Which is the Plaza and which is the Grand? What do Wilma and Fred say about the two hotels? Read their sentences. Then listen again and fill in the gaps with the comparative adjectives in the Word Box.

nicer✓	friendlier	bigger	more expensive
cleaner	better	worse	more comfortable

Example: The Plaza Hotel is <u>nicer</u> than /ðən/ the Grand Hotel.

1 The Grand is .... now than it was three years ago.
2 The rooms at the Plaza are .... and ....
than the rooms at the Grand.
3 The food at the Plaza is .... than the food at the Grand.
4 The beach near the Plaza is .... than the beach near
the Grand.
5 The market is .... than the little shop by the church.
6 The people at the little shop by the church are .... than
the people in the market.

2 a) Look again at your answers to Exercise 1b) and then fill in the gaps
in the Language Box on the right.

b) Write the comparative forms of the adjectives in the table below.

Comparative adjectives

There are five different forms of comparative adjectives.

1 short adjectives (one syllable):
+ -*er*
<u>cleaner</u>
....

2 short adjectives with one vowel
and consonant at the end:
double consonant + -*er*.

....

3 adjectives with a vowel and -*y*
at the end: -*y* → -*i* + -*er*

....

4 long adjectives (two or more
syllables): *more* + adjective

....
....
....

5 irregular adjectives:
bad → <u>worse</u>, *good* → <u>better</u>

....

Adjective	Comparative	Adjective	Comparative
bad	worse	easy	....
beautiful	....	expensive	....
boring	....	fast	....
busy	....	good	....
cheap	....	interesting	....
clean	....	lovely	....
comfortable	....	polite	....
crowded	....	rude	....
difficult	....	ugly	....

3 Fred is talking to Terry. What do you think he says? Use the words in
the Word Box.

my car	my wife	my job	fast	good	interesting	expensive
my house	my camera		intelligent	beautiful	big	difficult

Example: My car is faster than your car.

4 In pairs. Use the adjectives in Exercise 2b) and talk about the
town / city where you live. Think about the cinemas, hotels,
restaurants, shops and buildings. Make comparative sentences.

Example: The Classic cinema is more expensive than the Roxy.

Not as + adjective + as

5 a) Read the Language Box below and make four sentences about the two hotels. Use *not as* /əz/ + adjective + *as* /əz/.

> ### Not as + adjective + as
>
> We can also make comparative sentences with *isn't / aren't as* + adjective + *as*.
> The Grand **isn't as big as** the Plaza. = The Plaza is bigger than the Grand.

Example: The receptionists at the Grand / not polite / the receptionists at the Plaza.
The receptionists at the Grand aren't as polite as the receptionists at the Plaza.

1 The pool at the Plaza / not crowded / the pool at the Grand.
2 The shop at the Grand / not cheap / the shop at the Plaza.
3 The manager of the Grand / not friendly / the manager of the Plaza.
4 The restaurant at the Grand / not big / the restaurant at the Plaza.

b) 🔊 84 Listen and check.

c) Change the sentences in Exercise 5a). Use comparative adjectives.

Example: The receptionists at the Plaza are more polite than the receptionists at the Grand.

Prepositions of place: *Where's . . . ?*

6 a) 🔊 85 Terry and Debbie are at reception in the Plaza Hotel. They're meeting Fred and Wilma in the restaurant. Look at the plan of the ground floor of the hotel and read the conversation. Then listen and fill in the gaps with words from the Word Box.

> opposite ✔   on the left (x 2)
> on the right   next to (x 3)

TERRY: Where's the restaurant, please?
RECEPTIONIST: It's just down the corridor .... , <u>opposite</u> the lift.
TERRY: Thank you. And is there a shop in the hotel? My wife wants to buy a film for her camera.
RECEPTIONIST: Yes. It's down the corridor, ... It's .... the café.
TERRY: Right. Thanks. And I need to make a phone call. Is there a telephone, please?
RECEPTIONIST: It's just there, ... the lift.
TERRY: Thanks very much.
RECEPTIONIST: You're welcome.
DEBBIE: Excuse me. Um, where's the toilet?
RECEPTIONIST: It's down the corridor, ... , ... the bar.
DEBBIE: Thank you.

b) What are the places (a–d) on the plan?

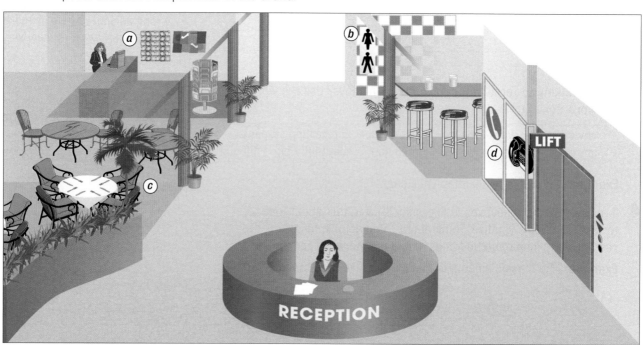

Advertisements

7 a) In pairs. Look at the magazine advertisements (ads). What products are they advertising? Match three adjectives from the Word Box to each product.

> young   delicious   easy   soft   beautiful   quick

b) 🔊 86 Listen to the radio ads for the same products and check.

c) 🔊 86 What do the people in the ads say? Listen again and finish their sentences. Use the comparative forms of the adjectives in the Word Box in Exercise 7a).

1 a) I look ....
   b) My skin feels ....
   c) I'm more ....

2 a) They're ....
   b) They're ....
   c) They're more ....

8 a) In groups, design a product for a radio ad and think about these questions.

1 What kind of product is it? A beauty / health / cleaning product, food, a business, a course, a car?
2 What is the name of your product?
3 What are three good things about it?

b) Plan your radio ad. Think about these questions.

1 What is the situation?
2 Who are the people?
3 What three things are you saying about your product? Use comparative adjectives. Remember, everyone in your group must say something in the ad.

c) Before you act out your ad, think of three questions to ask the class about your product. Then act out your ad and try to sell your product. Ask the class your questions.

Grammar reference and puzzles
Comparative adjectives: page 109

1 Classroom madness!

Look at the students (1–7) in the picture. Match one adjective from the Word Box to each student.

> lazy selfish polite shy
> sweet sporty stupid

2 Shopping trolleys

In pairs. Student A, look at page 117 and Student B at page 119.

3 *When are they doing that?*

a) Write questions with *who* and *when*.

Example: go / to Rome?
Who's going to Rome?
When is . . . going to Rome?

1 have / a driving lesson?
2 go / to a wedding?
3 play / golf?
4 get / married?
5 go / to the theatre?
6 fly / to Buenos Aires?
7 see / Tom?
8 meet / the bank manager?
9 drive / to Barcelona?
10 have / an Italian test?
11 meet / Sue?

b) In groups of four. Student A, look at page 116; Student B at page 118; Student C at page 121 and Student D at page 122.

4 Comparing places

a) [OO] 87 Phil went to Australia for his last holiday. Listen to him comparing Australia with England and underline the adjectives he uses in the Word Box.

> big ✓ polite crowded cheap interesting
> expensive friendly clean attractive rude bad
> nice exciting beautiful dirty good warm sweet

b) Now finish his sentences.

Example: Australia is much bigger than England.

1 It's .... and ....
2 The people are ....
3 The shop assistants are ....
4 The weather is .... and ....
5 The centre of Sydney is .... than the centre of London and it isn't as ....
6 The women are .... and ....

c) Use the adjectives in Exercise 4a) and compare two towns / cities you know.

> Look at the Word lists for Units 9–12 on pages 135–136 and check that you know all the new words.

Speech bubbles: No. I didn't do the homework. / Excuse me. Can I close the window? / Er! I don't know. / You can sit here. / Sorry, this is my table. / Er . . . sorry . . .

Wavelength page

Reading for pleasure

⑥ *Family life*

On the same Wavelength and other stories
LONGMAN   Elaine O'Reilly

1 "Family Life" is an American sit-com. This episode is called "Thanksgiving" – a very special family holiday on the last Thursday in November. Americans first celebrated Thanksgiving more than two hundred years ago. Before you read the story, what do you think they celebrated?

1 Christopher Columbus's arrival in America in 1492.
2 The end of the European settlers' first year in America when they sat down to eat with the Native Americans.
3 The first battle the European settlers won against the Native Americans.

2 🔊 88 Read and listen to the first part of the story. Then answer the questions.

1 What kind of book is Donna reading?
2 Do you think Donna is an experienced cook?
3 Who phones her?
4 Who is coming to have Thanksgiving dinner with her?
5 Why does Donna say "Oh, no!"?

3 Before you read the whole story, how do you think Donna will solve the problem of the frozen turkey?

1 She'll go out and buy a cooked turkey.
2 Her friends will help her with the dinner.
3 Her mother will arrive and do all the cooking.

4 Now read the whole story. It starts on page 20 of *On the same wavelength and other stories*. Think about these questions while you read.

1 How does Donna try to defrost the turkey at first?
2 Who comes to visit her?
3 Is Ricardo an experienced cook?
4 Does Ricardo know about Thanksgiving? Why / Why not?
5 What suggestion does he make about defrosting the turkey?
6 Where does he go then? Why?
7 What does he bring back from the supermarket?
8 Who cooks Donna's turkey and makes the stuffing?
9 When Donna's family arrive, her mother is carrying something. What is it?
10 How does Donna react at first? At the end?
11 Who opens the bottle of champagne?
12 Who do they drink a toast to?

Donna Hoffman

"Family Life" is a sit-com about a typical American family, the Hoffmans and their friends and neighbors. Donna, the 20-year-old daughter, recently went to live on her own. Her parents don't like it, but Donna wants to be independent.

Episode 492: Thanksgiving

CAST

Donna Hoffman
Rose Hoffman, her mother
Sam Hoffman, her father
Buddy Hoffman, her 14-year-old brother
Ricardo Santos, her Brazilian neighbor
Mrs. Macdonald, another neighbor

Donna is sitting at the kitchen table. She's wearing jeans and a T-shirt. She has a big book open in front of her. In a close-up we see the title: "The Fun of Cooking".

DONNA: Who says that cooking is fun? I don't even understand the words . . .

The phone rings. She gets up to answer it.

DONNA: Hello? Oh, hi Mom. *(pause)* And Happy Thanksgiving to you too. *(pause)* No, no, everything's OK. *(pause)* Mom, I said everything's OK! *(pause)* No, the turkey's not in the oven yet. It's in . . . *(She closes her eyes in horror.)* Mom I can't talk now! What time are you all coming? *(pause)* Can we make that three o'clock? I'm running late . . . OK, 'bye Mom. *(pause)* No, just say Happy Thanksgiving to him for me. See you at three.

Donna puts down the phone and goes to the big refrigerator. She opens the freezer section . . . the camera moves in to show us the turkey – it's still frozen!

DONNA: Oh, no! *(fade)*

13 Life stories

Present Perfect

Positive and negative sentences

1 a) Look at the photograph and read the beginning of the article on the right. What are people afraid of?

b) 🔟 89 Listen to two people talking about their fears. What are they afraid of?

c) What are you afraid of? Go round the class and ask students about the things in the table. Make notes about the answers.

2 a) Read the rest of the article on page 81. What are Karen White, Jean-Paul Dupré and Claudia Schmidt afraid of?

b) Where do these sentences go? Fill in the gaps in the article with the numbers of the sentences (1–3).

1 But I've been in only one really frightening situation.
2 My brother has had two really frightening experiences with dogs.
3 I've been stuck in a lift twice in my life.

c) Fill in the table about their experiences.

Who?	Experiences
Claudia	has lived in Tokyo.
1	has climbed Mount Everest.
2	has driven across the Sahara Desert.
3	has been to Asia.

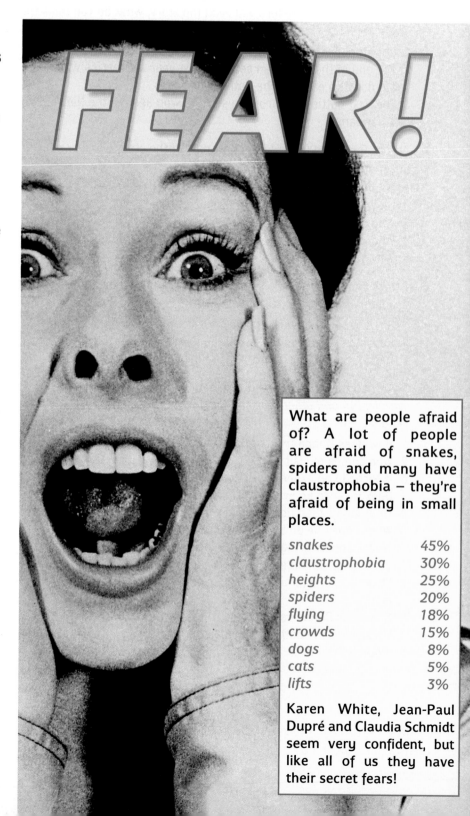

What are people afraid of? A lot of people are afraid of snakes, spiders and many have claustrophobia – they're afraid of being in small places.

snakes	45%
claustrophobia	30%
heights	25%
spiders	20%
flying	18%
crowds	15%
dogs	8%
cats	5%
lifts	3%

Karen White, Jean-Paul Dupré and Claudia Schmidt seem very confident, but like all of us they have their secret fears!

3 Read the Language Box on the right. Then underline all the Present Perfect verbs in the article. Which past participles are regular? Which are irregular?

Present Perfect

We use *have / has* + the past participle.

Positive

Subject	Have	Past participle
I / you / we / they he / she / it	've (have) 's (has)	worked.

Negative

Subject	Have	Past participle
I / you / we / they he / she / it	haven't (have not) hasn't (has not)	worked.

Look!
- *Been* or *gone*?
  Claudia **has been** to China but she's in Geneva now.
  Karl **has gone** to China and he's in China now.

Karen White
Mountain climber

Karen has climbed Mount Everest three times, but she isn't always brave.

"My boyfriend David, lives on the tenth floor of a block of flats but I always walk up the stairs when I visit him. Why? I hate lifts. .... The first time was in my grandmother's block of flats when I was a child. It was very frightening. I was stuck in the lift for half an hour and nobody knew. The second time was six years ago. The lift in my office building stopped between floors – I was alone again and it was completely dark. Both times I was very frightened and now I just can't get into a lift. I've lived in four different flats but they've all been on the ground floor."

Karen White, London

Jean-Paul Dupré
Photo-journalist

Jean-Paul loves adventure but his sister, Sophie, writes about his secret fear.

"...................... . The first was when he was five years old. He was alone in the garden at home and our neighbour's dog bit him three times. Two years later we had a holiday on a farm in England and the farmer's dog attacked him. Jean-Paul was very frightened both times and now he hates dogs. He can't go near them. He isn't usually frightened and he loves adventure. He has worked in some very lonely places. He has driven across the Sahara Desert from Morocco to Egypt. He has travelled alone many times. He has been to about forty different countries. Last year he visited Colombia and Peru. And he went to Brazil and Argentina. He does a lot of dangerous sports – he has broken his leg three times. Jean-Paul hasn't told many of his friends about his fear of dogs because he doesn't like talking about it."

*Sophie Dupré, **Paris***

Claudia Schmidt
United Nations researcher

Claudia Schmidt is afraid of flying. She tells us why.

"I've travelled a lot for my job and I love it. My husband, Karl, and I work for the United Nations. We've been to South America, Asia and parts of Africa because of our work. Karl's in China now. We've lived in Nairobi, Paris and Tokyo. I've met a lot of famous people and I've seen a lot of interesting places. I've been in planes hundreds of times. .... I was on a flight to Hong Kong two years ago. The plane had engine trouble – it almost crashed. Everyone on the plane was very frightened. I still travel a lot but I sometimes feel nervous when I fly."

Claudia Schmidt, Geneva

4 a) Karen, the mountain climber and her boyfriend, David, have had some wonderful holidays. Look at the postcards and make sentences about them.

Example: Karen and David / go / to Peru
1 They've been to Peru.

2 Karen and David / go / on safari in Kenya
3 Karen / climb / the Matterhorn in Switzerland
4 David / cycle / across the USA
5 Karen and David / visit / the Alhambra in Spain
6 Karen and David / go / India
7 Karen and David / travel / down the River Danube
8 Karen / go / scuba diving in Australia

b) Now match the sentences (1–8) from exercise 4a) to the postcards (a–h).

Example: 1 = a)

c) Now make negative sentences about Karen and David.

Example: 1 Mexico
They've been to Peru but they haven't been to Mexico.

2 Tanzania   6 China
3 K2   7 The Nile
4 South America 8 The Caribbean
5 The Eiffel Tower

Yes / No questions and short answers

5 In pairs. Make questions and answer them.

Example: 1 Jean-Paul / go / to Egypt?
Has Jean-Paul been to Egypt?
Yes, he has.

2 Claudia and Karl / live / Japan?
3 Jean-Paul / drive across / USA?
4 Karen / climb / Kilimanjaro?
5 Claudia and Karl / go / Australia?

Present Perfect or Past Simple?

6 **a)** In pairs. Read these sentences. Which two sentences talk about a definite time in the past?

Present Perfect

He has worked in some very lonely places.

Past Simple

Last year he visited Colombia and Peru.

Present Perfect

I've been in planes hundreds of times.

Past Simple

I was on a flight to Hong Kong two years ago.

b) Find sentences about a definite time in the past in the article about fear.

Pronunciation: Present Perfect or Past Simple?

7 🔊 90 Listen and tick (✓) the sentence you hear.

Example: a) I've worked in France. ✔ b) I worked in France. ☐

1 a) They've climbed Mount Everest. ☐   b) They climbed Mount Everest. ☐
2 a) He's lived in Brazil. ☐   b) He lived in Brazil. ☐
3 a) I've travelled a lot. ☐   b) I travelled a lot. ☐
4 a) She's travelled in India. ☐   b) She travelled in India. ☐

Have you ever . . . ?

8 **a)** Read Dave and Phil's conversation and fill in the gaps.

DAVE: .... you ever .... to Australia?   PHIL: Yes, I ....
DAVE: Really? When .... you .... ?   PHIL: Three months ago.
DAVE: How long .... you .... ?   PHIL: I stayed for a month.
DAVE: Oh! Where ....?   PHIL: Sydney and Melbourne.
DAVE: What .... it like?   PHIL: Fantastic.

b) 🔊 91 Listen and check.

c) In pairs. Practise the conversation. Then change the information and talk about places you have been to.

d) In pairs. Have more conversations like the ones in Exercise 8a).

1 Have you ever been stuck in a lift?
2 Have you ever been really frightened?
3 Have you ever seen .... ?
4 Have you ever met .... ?

> *Grammar reference and puzzles*
> Present Perfect: page 110

Day to day English *Intonation*

Eating out

1 Look at the picture. Then read the conversation in Exercise 2 and answer the questions.

1 What do the man and woman order for starters and main courses?

2 How do they pay for their meal?

2 [oo] 92 Listen to the conversation. You'll hear it twice. In which conversation is the waiter polite? In which conversation is he rude?

WAITER: Are you ready to order?

WOMAN: Um, what's Pascal's ravioli exactly?

WAITER: Well, it's ravioli with spinach in cheese sauce.

WOMAN: I see. Right. Well, for a starter I'd like the soup. And then the chicken, please, with a green salad.

MAN: And I'd like the lamb and some vegetables, please.

WAITER: And what would you like to drink?

MAN: We'd like the house wine.

WAITER: Red or white?

MAN: Red, please.

WAITER: Would you like a dessert?

MAN: Um, no, thank you.

WOMAN: Yes, please. I'd like fresh fruit salad.

WAITER: Certainly. Anything else? Coffee?

WOMAN: Yes, please. Two coffees.

MAN: Excuse me. Can we have the bill?

WAITER: Yes, just a moment.

MAN: Do you take Visa?

WAITER: Yes, we do.

3 In groups of three. Take it in turns to be the customers and a waiter. Decide if you are polite or rude. Use the menu and have conversations like the one in Exercise 2.

Pascal's

MENU

STARTERS

French onion soup	£5.50
Prawns with garlic	£8.75
Vegetable platter	£7.00
Smoked chicken salad	£6.75

MAIN COURSES

Fresh Scottish salmon with lemon sauce	£14.00
Pascal's ravioli	£11.50
Grilled chicken with rice	£12.00
Roast lamb with garlic	£12.75
Spaghetti with roasted vegetables	£10.20

VEGETABLES

Fresh vegetables (potatoes, carrots, beans)	£4.00
Green salad	£3.50

DESSERTS

Chocolate cake	£4.75
Fresh fruit salad	£4.75
Cheese and biscuits	£4.00

For Today's Specials, please look at the board.

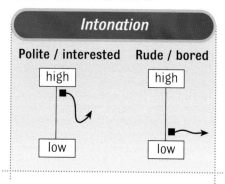

Intonation

Polite / interested	Rude / bored
high	high
low	low

Perfect places

Describing places
Prepositions of place: *Where . . . ?*
My favourite place
Skills: Visit the East End!

Describing places

1 a) Look at the views (1–5). Which view do you like best? What can you see? Use the words in the Word Box.

wall	a beach	buildings /ˈbɪldɪŋz/	purple	a forest
the sea	windows	trees	grey	sand	a garden
plant pots	hills	a river	mountains /ˈmaʊntɪns/	
reflection /rɪˈflekʃən/	the sky	grass	a lake	
sunset	flowers	boat	clouds	fields	snow

b) [oo] 93 Listen to Paul. Which view is he describing?

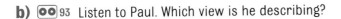

2 🔊 93 Listen again. Use the words from the Word Box in Exercise 1a) and fill in the gaps in Paul's description. Then read the Language Box on the right.

This is a view of New York. It's very exciting. It's .... and .... is .... , yellow and orange. There are some grey .... too. I can see some tall buildings. There are a lot of lights in the .... In the centre there's a very tall building. It's the Empire State Building. In the distance there's .... It's the Hudson River.

3 a) Write a description of one of the other views from Exercise 1a). Don't say which view you are writing about. Make one mistake in your description.

b) In groups. Take it in turns to read each other's descriptions aloud. The group must guess which view the description is about and correct the mistake.

Example: You're describing view 2, but there aren't any trees!

4 🔊 94 Listen and imagine your own perfect view. Then in pairs. Take it in turns to describe them.

5 a) 🔊 95 Listen to six pieces of music and choose adjectives from the Word Box to describe them.

> calm   peaceful   exciting   happy
> lively   relaxing   dramatic   romantic

b) Choose a piece of music for your perfect view from Exercise 4. Then tell your partner about it.

Example: I want the second piece because my view is very calm and peaceful and this music is too.

Prepositions of place

6 Look at the map on the right and fill in the gaps with prepositions from the Word Box.

> on   near   in   between

Example: Naples is <u>on</u> the west coast of Italy.

1 Mount Vesuvius is .... Naples.
2 Ravello is .... the mountains.
3 Anacapri is .... the island of Capri.
4 Positano is .... Sorrento and Amalfi.
5 1,206,955 people live .... Naples.

> ## A or an, some and the
>
> The first time we talk about things we use:
> - **a / an** for singular nouns. (But we always use **the** with these nouns: *the sun, the sea, the moon, the sky.*)
>
> We use
> - **some** for plural countable nouns and uncountable nouns.
>
> The next time we talk about them we use **the** or a **pronoun** (*he, she, it, they*).

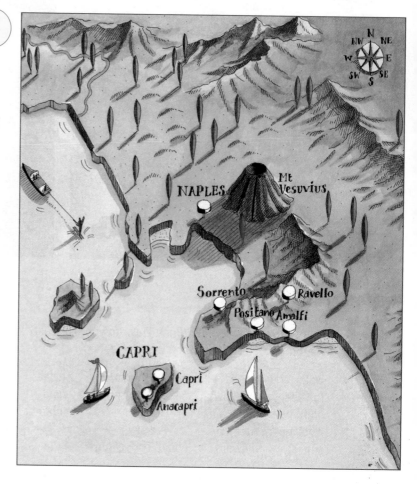

My favourite place

7 In pairs. Read the instructions.

Student A: Look at the magazine article below. Read Sue's description of her favourite place. Fill in the table about Sue. Then ask Student B questions and fill in the table about Matt.

Student B: Look at the magazine article on page 88. Read Matt's description of his favourite place. Fill in the table about Matt. Then ask Student A questions and fill in the table about Sue.

Sue

One of my best travel memories is when my family and I stayed on an island called Tioman. It's a tiny island in the South China Sea near the east coast of Malaysia. We went there two years ago because my sister lived in Malaysia at the time. It's very, very beautiful – paradise. It's a tropical island with lovely beaches, huge palm trees and lots of different types of sweet-smelling tropical flowers, like frangipani. Inland there's the jungle and some huge mountains. It's where they made the film *South Pacific* in the 1950s. The sea is amazing – very, very blue – dark blue. You can look down and see hundreds of different coloured tropical fish – red, yellow, green, pink, blue . . . The island is tiny. It's so small that you can walk across the middle part in half a day. There are only three or four villages and one hotel. The hotel is right on the beach. We could hear the sound of the sea at night when we were in bed. One day I want to go back . . .

	Sue	Matt
1 What's the name of the place?	....	....
2 Where is it?	....	....
	....	....
3 When did they first go there?	....	....
4 Is it a big place?	....	....
5 What's the countryside like?	....	....
	....	....
	....	....
6 Why do they love this place?	....	....
	....	....
	....	....

My favourite place is Kinsale. It's a small fishing village on the south coast of Ireland, near a city called Cork. I live in London but my parents live in Cork. They moved there about five years ago – that's when I first went to Kinsale. When I visit them in Cork I always go to Kinsale. There are lots of small, interesting pubs and colourful houses. The local beer is called Murphy's. It's like Guinness but much better because it comes from Cork! What I really love about Kinsale is the scenery. The countryside is very green, with gentle hills. It's very peaceful and relaxing. There's an old fort called Charles Fort about three miles from the village. There are beautiful views from there. You can see miles of beautiful coastline, the Atlantic Ocean and then . . . on a clear day . . . America! The other thing I love about Kinsale is the air – it's so fresh and clear. I really need that fresh air after the pollution in London.

Matt

	Matt	Sue
1 What's the name of the place?		
2 Where is it?		
3 When did they first go there?		
4 Is it a big place?		
5 What's the countryside like?		
6 Why do they love this place?		

8 a) 🔊 96 Listen. Sue and Matt are talking to each other about Tioman and Kinsale. Write their questions. Then listen again and make notes about their answers.

b) Compare the two places. Which do you like more? Why?

The perfect place

9 a) Use the questions from Exercise 8a) and write a description of a place that you know and love.

b) In groups of three. Read each others' descriptions. Ask more questions to find out about the places.

Skills Reading, writing

1 a) Fill in the gaps with words from the Word Box.

> bargain✓ /ˈbɑːgɪn/ (n)
> immigrants (n pl)
> second-hand (adj)
> furniture /ˈfɜːnɪtʃə/

Example: I bought this coat for only £5. It was a real bargain.

1 My car isn't new. I bought it ....

2 My boss has a lot of beautiful .... in his house.

3 .... from all over the world live in England.

b) Read the brochure quickly. Answer these questions.

1 Where is the East End?
2 Who lives there?
3 How many markets are in the brochure?
4 Can you only eat British food in the East End?

c) Some people are visiting the East End. Read the brochure again and make suggestions.

Example: A: I love Asian food, especially curries.
B: What about going to the Clifton restaurant?

1 I'm looking for a new jacket.
2 I'd like a beer in a typical London pub.
3 Where can we see some famous people?
4 I'm looking for cheap CDs.

2 a) Betty came to London to visit her daughter, and they went to the East End. Betty made four mistakes in her letter. Find them and correct them.

b) Imagine that a friend took you to the East End. Write a letter to thank him / her.

VISIT THE EAST END!

The East End of London is a rich mix of different cultures and people. This area, next to the River Thames, the docks and the City (the financial centre of London) is home to Cockneys, artists, designers, people who work in the City and immigrants to Britain.

Markets

Three of the best are:

PETTICOAT LANE: Open every day except Saturday. The market has new clothes, including designer fashion – great bargains!

COLUMBIA ROAD: Open on Sunday 8:00–14:00. A lively market for flowers and plants. Very cheap – £2.00–£5.00 for a plant!

SPITALFIELDS MARKET: Open every day except Saturday. This large market has restaurants, a leisure centre and a swimming pool as well as stalls selling second-hand clothes, records and CDs, posters, organic food, jewellery, perfume and furniture.

Food and drink

The East End is famous for its pubs and food, especially curries, bagels and Cockney jellied eels.

THE BRICK LANE BAGEL BAKE: They sell hot fresh bagels twenty-four hours a day. You can sometimes see the rich and famous enjoying a late night snack!

THE CLIFTON RESTAURANT: Cheap tasty food from Bangladesh and India – great curries.

THE PALM TREE: A typical East End pub – friendly and lively. On Saturday and Sunday there is live music.

And if you want to relax . . .

YORK HALL: Try a Turkish Bath and a massage.

Wavelength page

Dear Kathy,

Well, I finally got back! It's good to be home but I really enjoyed my week with you – and I loved our Sunday in the West End. Thank you so much for having me.

Yesterday I cooked a curry! I remember the chicken curry we had at the Palm Tree. It was delicious – but very hot. Jenny loves her T-shirt. She's wearing it now. And it only cost £3.50! Petticoat Lane really is cheaper than the shops here.

And how's the plant I bought you in Columbia Road? I can't believe I only paid £20 for it! How's it doing? Oh, and what about the Roman Baths? I felt fantastic when I came out – really relaxed and clean. When I'm here I never have time to relax!

Anyway, thanks for a wonderful week.

Love,
Mum

Reading for pleasure

⑦ The real thing

1 This is the story of two men and a beautiful drawing by Leonardo da Vinci. Before you read it, are these questions about Leonardo da Vinci true (T) of false (F)? Try to correct the false sentences.

Example: He painted the "Mona Lisa". ☐T☐

1 He was Spanish. ☐
2 He was also a scientist and an engineer. ☐
3 There are more of his drawings than his paintings left. ☐
4 He lived in the nineteenth century. ☐

2 👓97 Read and listen to the first part of the story. Then answer the questions.

1 Which of the men was older – Pickering or Bromfield?
2 Why do you think Sebastian was so nervous?
3 What was Mr Pickering an expert on?
4 Sebastian made a mistake that Mr Pickering corrected. What was it?
5 Where do you think Sebastian's drawing was?

3 Before you read the whole story, what do you think happened next?

1 Sebastian tried to sell his drawing to Mr Pickering.
2 Mr Pickering told Sebastian that his drawing was worth very little money.
3 Mr Pickering tried to steal Sebastian's drawing.

4 Now read the whole story. It starts on page 24 of *On the same wavelength and other stories*. Think about these questions while you read.

1 What was Sebastian's drawing of?
2 Where did he say he got the drawing?
3 What did Pickering say about the drawing?
4 Why was Pickering sure the drawing was a copy?
5 Pickering compared his drawing and Sebastian's drawing. How were they different?
6 How much did Pickering say Sebastian's drawing was worth?
7 How did Sebastian react?
8 What did Sebastian do when he left Pickering's office?
9 Where did he tell the driver to go? Why?
10 What was in his briefcase at the end?

The two men stood on opposite sides of the large desk. The older man was tall and handsome. He had a fine head of silver hair and his eyes were blue but very cold.

The young man was also tall. His hair was long and blonde – he had the clear eyes and open face of a boy and his smile was shy. He had an old brown leather briefcase under his arm. He was very, very nervous.

The older man was the first to speak. "Sit down, Mr . . . um . . ."

"Bromfield. Sebastian Bromfield. It's very kind of you to see me, Mr Pickering."

"I don't have much time, Mr Bromfield. What can I do for you?"

"Mr Pickering, they say you are an expert on Leonardo da Vinci . . ."

The older man corrected Sebastian's pronunciation of the great painter's name. Sebastian blushed and continued.

"Sorry, yes, of course. Well, I have a drawing . . . and I think, that perhaps, I mean . . . maybe it's by Leonardo da Vinci." This time he said the name correctly.

"Really?" Pickering laughed coldly. "And where is this drawing?"

"I have it here. Just a minute . . ."

15 So how are you feeling today?

Illnesses
Feelings
Linkers: *because* and *so*
Conversations: *Oh, I know . . .*

Illnesses

1 a) Look at the picture. It's the night before the *Song for the World* competition. Singers from all over the world are competing. What do you think is wrong with the singers? Match the singers (1–8) to the illnesses (a–h).

Example: 1 = f)

b) 🔊 98 Listen and check.

c) 🔊 99 Listen and repeat.

a) I've got a hangover.
b) I've got a stomachache.
c) I've got a cough.
d) I've got a toothache.
e) I've got a temperature.
f) I've got a cold.
g) I've got a headache.
h) I've got a sore throat.

2 a) Read this questionnaire. Use the verbs in the Word Box and fill in the gaps. Then write one more possible question for each problem.

> do ✓ go (x 5) close take (x 4) eat (x 2)
> lie (x 2) phone smoke drink

─\/─You and your health─\/─

Do you look after yourself?

	You	Your partner
1 You've got a headache. Do you a) _do_ nothing? b) .... an aspirin? c) .... to bed immediately? d) .... ?	☐ ☐ ☐ ☐	☐ ☐ ☐ ☐
2 You've got a sore throat. Do you a) .... to the doctor's immediately? b) .... the windows and turn up the heating? c) .... another cigarette? d) .... ?	☐ ☐ ☐ ☐	☐ ☐ ☐ ☐
3 You've got a cold and a cough. Do you a) .... some cough medicine? b) .... a lot of vitamin C tablets? c) .... out and give your cold to everybody? d) .... ?	☐ ☐ ☐ ☐	☐ ☐ ☐ ☐
4 You've got a stomachache. Do you a) .... for an ambulance? b) .... down on the floor and relax? c) .... a big meal? d) .... ?	☐ ☐ ☐ ☐	☐ ☐ ☐ ☐
5 You've got a toothache. Do you a) .... a bottle of whisky? b) .... to the dentist? c) .... a bar of chocolate? d) .... ?	☐ ☐ ☐ ☐	☐ ☐ ☐ ☐
6 You've got a temperature. Do you a) .... in a bath of cold water for two hours? b) .... two aspirins? c) .... dancing in a crowded nightclub? d) .... ?	☐ ☐ ☐ ☐	☐ ☐ ☐ ☐

b) In pairs. Take it in turns to ask each other the questions and fill in the questionnaire. Then compare your answers and talk about these questions.

1 Do you and your partner do the same things or different things when you're ill?

2 Do you know any traditional cures for these problems?

Feelings

3 a) 🔊 100 Charlie's fed up. Last week was terrible for him. Three bad things happened to him. Look at the pictures (1–4) and listen. Tick (✓) the three things that happened.

b) 🔊 100 Listen again and finish the sentences.

1 He was depressed because . . .
2 He was angry because . . .
3 He was tired because . . .

Linkers: *because* and *so*

4 Read the Language Box below. Then fill in the gaps with *because, so* or *why*.

> ### Because, so and why
>
> • Charlie was angry **because** his brother crashed his car.
>   (result)   (reason)
> • His brother crashed Charlie's car **so** Charlie was angry.
>   (reason)   (result)
> • We use *why* in questions.
>   **Why** was Charlie angry?

Example: He's depressed <u>because</u> he failed his exam.

1 I'm tired .... I'm not playing football tomorrow.
2 Sonia heard a strange noise outside last night. She was really frightened .... she phoned the police.
3 A: .... did he break the plate?
   B: .... he was angry.
4 He's fed up .... his job is very boring. He does the same things every day.
5 He had a headache .... he took two aspirins.

5 a) Write two sentences about yourself or a person you know for each feeling in Exercise 3b).

Examples: I was tired last Tuesday **so** I didn't go to college.
               I was tired **because** I went to a party on Monday night.

b) In groups. Talk about your sentences from Exercise 5a).

Example: A: I was tired last Tuesday so I didn't go to college.
          B: Why were you tired?
          A: Because I went to a party on Monday night.

A taste of paradise

Introductory day for only £100!

Feeling stressed out? Need a break? Fed up?

Our introductory day at Paradise Hall is perfect for people who don't have a lot of time. These special days start at 10 a.m. and finish at 8 p.m.

You can have:
- a massage
- a facial
- a sauna

You can also:
- swim in the indoor and outdoor pools
- use the gym
- play golf and tennis
- do yoga
- go fishing and biking

The price also includes lunch in our relaxing Garden Café and your evening meal in the beautiful Shangri-la Restaurant.

Let's get away from it all!

6 Charlie went to Paradise Hall after his terrible week. Read the brochure and look at the pictures of Charlie (1–4). What did he do?

7 In pairs. Have you ever been to a place like Paradise Hall? Would you like to go? Ask your partner about the things in the brochure.

Example:
A: Have you ever had a facial?
B: Yes, I have.
A: What was it like?
B: It was really relaxing. First . . . and then . . .

8 You're going to Paradise Hall for one day. Look at the brochure and organise your day from 10 a.m. to 8 p.m. Then in groups, take it in turns to describe your day.

Example: At 10:00 I'm playing tennis. Then at 11:00 I'm having a massage. At 12:00 I'm going to the gym and then at 1:00 I'm . . .

①

②

③

④

1 **a)** In pairs. Look at Pictures a) and b). Which of the sentences (1–6) go with Picture a) and which go with Picture b)? Put the sentences in the correct order.

1 Oh? Where did you go?
2 Oh, I know what you mean!
3 Why? What happened?
4 No, I went out.
5 Oh, I had a bad headache when I woke up. I really need a holiday.
6 Oh, I just went to a friend's house.

b) **[oo]** 101 Listen and check. Then in pairs, practise the conversations.

2 Match each sentence in A with two sentences from B. Then in pairs, practise the conversations.

Example: 1 = b) or e)
  A: I'm studying Spanish at the moment.
  B: Really? Is it difficult?
  OR
  A: I'm studying Spanish at the moment.
  B: Oh, I love Spanish. I lived in Spain for a year.

A
1 I'm studying Spanish at the moment.
2 I want to go to the Grand Canyon this summer.
3 That shop is really expensive.

B
a) Yeah, I know. I never go there.
b) Really? Is it difficult?
c) Yes, I know what you mean, but it has some nice things.
d) Oh, I've been there. It's amazing.
e) Oh, I love Spanish. I lived in Spain for a year.
f) But you don't have any money.

3 **a)** Read the Language Box on the right. Then in pairs, choose a starter sentence (1–3) and plan a four-line conversation.

Example: A: I get up early for work.
    B: **Really!** I hate getting up early.
    A: **Yeah, I know what you mean.** Especially in winter when it's cold and dark.
    B: **Oh, yeah.** I don't like cold weather. I always go to a warm country on holiday. I've been to Greece six times.

1 I spent a lot of money at the weekend.
2 Have you ever been to an aerobics class?
3 I'm reading a great book at the moment.

b) In groups of four. Listen to each other's conversations. Then choose a different starter sentence. This time each student adds a line.

Keeping a conversation going

We can ask questions or add sentences to keep a conversation going.

Show interest / surprise
Really?

Continue with a similar idea
I know.
I know what you mean.
Yes / Yeah.
Have you ever . . . ?

Continue with a different idea
But . . .

Wavelength page

A look into the future

Want to do (dreams and ambitions) and
be going to do (intentions and plans)
Future plans
Do you remember? Units 13–16

Want to do and *be going to do*

1 In pairs. Talk about these questions.

1 Do you daydream on your way to school / college / work?
2 Do you daydream about your future?

2 a) Look at the picture of people on the Underground. What are they thinking about?

b) 🔊 102 Listen to the four people daydreaming about the future. Match the people to their daydreams.

Example: 1 = b)

c) 🔊 102 Listen again and fill in the gaps. Then read the Language Box on the right.

1 I really .... get away and relax.
  What .... to do?
  I'm going .... a holiday in the Seychelles.
2 I .... a motorbike.
  I .... a car.
  Where .... find the money?
3 Joe and I .... buy a new house.
  Joe .... live in the city.
  .... look at some houses tomorrow.
  But I'm .... tell Joe.
  I .... surprise him.
4 I .... something more exciting.
  I .... a nightclub singer.
  I'm going .... singing lessons next month.

Talking about the future

Dreams and ambitions
We often use *want to* + verb.

What do you **want to do**?
I **want to live** in the country.
I **don't want to buy** a motorbike.

Intentions and plans
We often use *be going to* + verb.

What's he **going to do**?
He's **going to buy** a sports car.
She **isn't going to tell** Joe.

3 Look at the table and make six sentences. Use the correct form of *want* and *be going to*.

Example: I want to learn to ski, so I'm going to have skiing lessons.

| I
We
They
He
She | **want to** | learn to ski
make more money
live in the country
travel
live by the sea
be healthier
learn to relax | **so** | I
we
they
he
she | **be going to . . .** |

4 Make sentences or questions with these words.

Example: your / to / job / leave / Why / are / going / you ?
         Why are you going to leave your job?

1 doesn't / boyfriend / want / Linda / on / to / with / holiday / go / her
2 going / Portuguese / study / daughter / Brazil / My / is / to / in
3 Phil / are / to / you / When / phone / going ?
4 look / Are / another / you / to / job / going / for ?
5 wants / husband / his / to / Her / job / change
6 to / they / go / Where / want / do ?

Pronunciation: *to*

5 **a)** We can say *to* in two different ways. Read the sentences and fill in the gaps in the Language Box below with /tuː/ or /tə/. Then practise the three sentences.

1 I'm going to /tə/ work for a travel agent's.
2 I'm going to /tuː/ open a shop.
3 He wants to go to /tə/ university.

> ### To: /tə/ or /tuː/?
>
> We say .... before a vowel sound and .... before a consonant.
>
> ***Look!***
> * *u* sometimes has the vowel sound /ʌ/ (*understand, Underground*) but sometimes sounds like a consonant: /juː/ (*university, use*).

b) Write 1 /tuː/ or 2 /tə/ in the box.

Example: I want to ☐2 /tə/ do something different.

1 He doesn't want to ☐ use the Underground.
2 When are you going to ☐ ask Linda?
3 I'm not going to ☐ move house.
4 Do you want to ☐ go?
5 Are you going to ☐ buy that house?

c) 🔊 103 Listen and check. Then listen again and repeat.

Future plans

6 **a)** On separate pieces of paper write three sentences about your future dreams and plans like the ones in Exercise 3.

Example: I want to go on holiday so I'm going to start saving money.

b) In groups of four. Put all your pieces of paper on the table. Take it in turns to pick up a piece of paper and guess who wrote the sentence. Ask questions about the sentences.

7 Look at the pictures (1–6). Why don't people like Phil? Make a sentence for each picture. Use the words in the Word Box.

> flirt with other women ✓   gossip about people
> arrive late   be selfish   borrow money
> lose his temper

Example: 1 He flirts with other women.

8 a) Look at the picture of Phil on the left. Why is he sad now?

b) How is Phil going to change? Use the words in the Word Box in Exercise 7 and make six sentences about Phil.

Example: 1 He isn't going to flirt with other women any more.

c) You want to be a better person. Make three sentences about yourself. Go round the class and talk to other students. Remember what they tell you.

Example: I'm not going to arrive late for my English lessons any more. What about you?

What do you want to do?
What are you going to do?

9 In groups of four. Student A, look at page 124; Student B at page 126; Student C at page 119 and Student D at page 123. Talk about what you want to do and what you're going to do.

Example: You're getting married next week. Last week you met someone new and you think you're in love. What do you want to do? What are you going to do?
> A: I want to tell the truth so I'm going to tell my boyfriend / girlfriend everything.
> or
> A: I don't want to hurt my family so I'm not going to say anything.
> or
> A: I want to be happy, so I'm going to move to another city with my new love. I'm not going to tell my family.
> or
> A: I want to choose the right person, so I'm going to go away for the weekend and think about it.

> **Grammar reference and puzzles**
> *Want to do* and *be going to do*: page 111

Wavelength page

1 Find the mistakes

a) In pairs. Look at the picture. What can you see in the picture?

b) 🔊 104 Listen to a woman talking about the picture. She makes six mistakes. What are they?

Example: 1 She says there's a woman in the sea but there's a man.

2 *What's the matter with him / her?*

a) Which words in the Word Box go with *be* and which go with *have / has got?* Make two lists.

> angry   sore throat   bored   cough   tired
> depressed   stomachache   hangover   temperature
> headache   fed up   frightened

b) In pairs. Use words from the Word Box in Exercise 2a) and write conversations about three different students in the class. Don't write their names.

Example: A: What's the matter with her?
B: She's tired.
A: Why?
B: Because she had a busy weekend.

c) In groups of four. Read your conversations and guess who the students are.

3 *Who's going to jump out of the balloon?*

a) In groups of six. You're all in a hot-air balloon. The balloon is going down quickly and two people must jump out. Think of two good things you've done in your life. Tell the group about them and answer their questions.

Example: A: I've helped a lot of people.
B: Who have you helped?
A: My brother.
C: When did you help him? What did you do?

b) Now make a list of four things you are going to do or not going to do in the future to be a better person. Take it in turns to read out your lists.

Example: I'm going to be friendlier. I'm not going to borrow money.

c) Who's going to jump out of the balloon? Write their names on a piece of paper and give them to your teacher.

Look at the Word lists for Units 13–16 on pages 136–137 and check that you know all the new words.

Reading for pleasure

⑧ Emergency!

1 This story happened in South Africa. Before 1991, South Africa had a white minority government. Which of these changes happened in 1991?

1 The police arrested Nelson Mandela and put him in prison.
2 The black majority voted for the first time.
3 Black people had the same rights as white people for the first time.

2 🔊 105 Read and listen to the first part of the story. Then answer the questions.

1 Was Zindzi at home?
2 Who were Piet and Gillie?
3 Where did Zindzi work?
4 Where did Piet and Gillie live?

3 What do you think happened next? What was the emergency?

1 Everyone went to bed. In the night Gillie was very ill but Zindzi saved her life.
2 Zindzi got a telephone call. She went out alone. She had a terrible accident.
3 Piet got a telephone call. He went out and left the two women alone in the house. Someone came into the house while they were sleeping.

4 Now read the whole story. It starts on page 28 of *On the same wavelength and other stories*. Think about these questions while you read.

1 What was Zindzi's job?
2 Why did Zindzi leave Piet and Gillie's house?
3 Why didn't Gillie want her to go?
4 Why did Zindzi drive slowly at first?
5 Why did she stop the car?
6 What did the old man do?
7 What language did he speak?
8 What happened when Zindzi's mobile phone rang?
9 Where did the old man get out of the car?
10 What did Zindzi do after the operation?
11 Who was in the waiting room with the boy's mother?

It was Sunday night. Zindzi sat by the swimming pool, listening to the noisy South African night. A concert of insects, frogs, night birds, baboons. In the distance, the sinister cough of a leopard.

"Something hot to drink before bed, Zindzi?" Gillie called from the veranda. "Piet and I are having some cocoa."

"No, not for me, thanks."

Zindzi watched Gillie go back into the house, followed by her fat old Labrador dog.

Zindzi loved spending time with Piet and Gillie. They were her dearest friends. They knew she worked hard at the hospital – she needed to relax at the weekend. Their big country house was her second home.

Grammar reference and puzzles

Be (Welcome pages: A and B)

Positive

Subject	*be*
I	'm (am)
You / We / They	're (are)
He / She / It	's (is)

Negative

Subject	*be*
I	'm not (am not)
You / We / They	aren't (are not)
He / She / It	isn't (is not)

Wh- questions

	be	Subject
Who	am	I?
	are	you / we / they?
	's (is)	he / she / it?

Yes / *No* questions

be	Subject	
Am	I	
Are	you / we / they	from Spain?
Is	he / she / it	

Look! No contractions.

Positive short answers

	Subject	*be*
Yes,	I	am.
	you / we / they	are.
	he / she / it	is.

Look! No contractions.

Negative short answers

	Subject	*be*
No,	I	'm not.
	you / we / they	aren't.
	he / she / it	isn't.

Secret place!

Find the secret word (people go there for a holiday).

Clues

1 The beach isn't clean. It's ....
2 A: Michael's from Ireland.
   B: .... he from Dublin?
3 A: Barry is American. Is he from California?
   B: No, he ....
4 A: Are you OK?
   B: No, I'm ....
5 I'm here on business. .... there any good restaurants near my hotel?
6 A: Is Dimitri Greek?
   B: ...., he is and he's really nice.
7 A: Is Marta nice?
   B: Oh, yes. She's ....
8 A: We're in Room 15.
   B: No, you're not. I ....
9 A: Is she married?
   B: ...., she's single.
10 A: I'm from Brazil. Are you from .... ?
    B: Yes, I'm from Montreal.

Present Simple (Units 1 and 2)

Positive

Subject	Verb
I / You / We / They	work.
He / She / It	works.

Negative

Subject	*do*	Verb
I / You / We / They	don't (do not)	work.
He / She / It	doesn't (does not)	

Wh- questions

	do	Subject	Verb
Where	do	I / you / we / they	work?
	does	he / she / it	

Yes / No questions

do	Subject	Verb
Do	I / you / we / they	work?
Does	he / she / it	

Positive short answers

	Subject	*do*
Yes,	I / you / we / they	do.
	he / she / it	does.

Negative short answers

	Subject	*do*
No,	I / you / we / they	don't.
	he / she / it	doesn't.

Form

Spelling

With *he, she, it* we usually add -*s* to positive verbs:

Simon works in a bank. **NOT** Simon work in a bank.

BUT

- add -*es* for verbs ending in -*o*, -*ch*, -*s*, -*sh* and -*x*:

  go → goes, teach → teaches, kiss → kisses, wash → washes, mix → mixes

- change -*y* to -*i* and add -*es* for verbs ending in a consonant + -*y*:

  study → studies, marry → marries, try → tries

- *have* changes to *has*:

  He has three sisters. **NOT** He have three sisters.

Use

Habits, routines, permanent situations

I usually get up late at the weekend.

He works for an advertising company.

With frequency adverbs

I **always** arrive on time.   100%

I **usually** arrive on time.

I **often** arrive on time.

I **sometimes** arrive on time.

I **hardly ever** arrive on time.

I **never** arrive on time.   0%

Secret job!

Find the secret words (a job).

Clues

1 He .... TV every day.
2 .... your boyfriend live in Spain?
3 She .... forty cigarettes a day.
4 Does he .... French well?
5 Do .... study at this college?
6 Felix always .... up late on Sunday morning.
7 John and Ann like Paris, so .... go there a lot.
8 I .... go to nightclubs. I don't like loud music.
9 Her children .... tennis every Saturday.
10 We like going to the cinema. We .... ever go to the theatre.
11 Susan .... work hard. She has a very easy job.
12 He .... to restaurants a lot. He hardly ever eats at home.
13 A journalist .... articles for newspapers.
14 She .... gets up early. She likes breakfast at 7 a.m.
15 Mat .... in the pool every morning.
16 He works in a hotel so he .... a lot of people.
17 Do you .... forget your family's birthdays?
18 .... do your parents live?

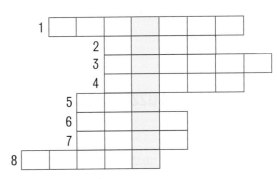

103

Present Continuous (Unit 4)

Positive

Subject	be	Verb + -ing
I	'm (am)	
You / We / They	're (are)	sleeping.
He / She / It	's (is)	

Negative

Subject	be	Verb + -ing
I	'm not (am not)	
You / We / They	aren't (are not)	sleeping.
He / She / It	isn't (is not)	

Wh- questions

	be	Subject	Verb + -ing
	am	I	
Where	are	you / we / they	sleeping?
	is	he / she / it	

Yes / No questions

be	Subject	Verb + -ing
Am	I	
Are	you / we / they	sleeping?
Is	he / she / it	

Positive short answers

	Subject	be
	I	am.
Yes,	you / we / they	are.
	he / she / it	is.

Negative short answers

	Subject	be
	I	'm not.
No,	you / we / they	aren't.
	he / she / it	isn't.

Form

Spelling

We usually add -ing to the verb:
read → reading, work → working

BUT

• verbs ending in a vowel + a consonant, double the consonant:
swim → swimming, rob → robbing
• verbs ending in -e, take off the -e:
have → having, make → making
• be changes to being.

Use

Activity happening now

PAST ← NOW → FUTURE

They're playing tennis
at the moment.

Compare the Present Continuous and the Present Simple:

PRESENT CONTINUOUS	PRESENT SIMPLE
Maria **is teaching** her class. (She is doing this now – at this moment.)	Maria **teaches** children in a school. (This is her job. She does it every day.)

Activity happening around now

I usually get up early.

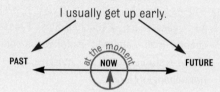

PAST ← at the moment NOW → FUTURE

But I'm getting up late
at the moment
because I'm on holiday.

Crossword puzzle

Clues

ACROSS

1 There aren't any seats, so she's .... (8)
6 I .... not sleeping very well these days. (2)
7 Are you .... your dictionary or can I use it? (5)
9 They are .... in a tent at the moment. (7)
11 I'm .... up at 6 a.m. at the moment. (7)

DOWN

2 Bella! Please stop .... and be quiet!' (7)
3 A: Are you learning Greek? B: Yes, I .... (2)
4 .... it snowing where you are? (2)
5 Be careful! You're .... too fast! (5)
8 What's he .... ? I can't hear! (6)
10 .... the children enjoying their holiday? (3)

Have got / has got and have / has (Unit 5)

Have got / has got

Positive

Subject	have		
I / You / We / They	've (have)	got	a job.
He / She / It	's (has)		

Negative

Subject	have		
I / You / We / They	haven't (have not)	got	a job.
He / She / It	hasn't (has not)		

Wh- questions

	have	Subject	
What	have	I / you / we / they	got?
	has	he / she / it	

Yes / No questions

have	Subject		
Have	I / you / we / they	got	a job?
Has	he / she / it		any pens?

Positive short answers

	Subject	have
Yes,	I / you / we / they	have.
	he / she / it	has.

Negative short answers

	Subject	have
No,	I / you / we / they	haven't.
	he / she / it	hasn't.

Have / has

Positive

Subject		
I / You / We / They	have	a job.
He / She / It	has	

Negative

Subject	have	
I / You / We / They	don't have (do not have)	a job.
He / She / It	doesn't have (does not have)	

Wh- questions

	do	Subject	
What	do	I / you / we / they	have?
	does	he / she / it	

Yes / No questions

do	Subject		
Do	I / you / we / they	have	a job?
Does	he / she / it		any pens?

Positive short answers

	Subject	do
Yes,	I / you / we / they	do.
	he / she / it	does.

Negative short answers

	Subject	do
No,	I / you / we / they	don't.
	he / she / it	doesn't.

Pyramid puzzle

Clues

1 Have you got .... car?
2 Has .... got his passport with him?
3 I haven't got .... cigarettes.
4 A: Have they got a swimming pool? B: Yes, they ....
5 A: Has their flat got a garden? B: No, it ....
6 Have we .... bananas? My monkey is hungry.
7 Do you want to listen to some music? I've .... CDs in the car.
8 .... got any children, so our house is very quiet.

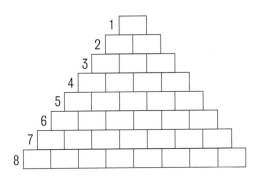

Past Simple (Units 6 and 7)

Regular and irregular verbs

Positive

Regular verbs	Subject	Past Simple
(ask)		asked
(arrive)		arrived
(marry)	I /	married
(stop)	you /	stopped
Irregular verbs	we /	
(see page 143)	they /	
(come)	he /	came
(go)	she /	went
(have)	it	had
(see)		saw

Negative

Subject	*do*	Verb
I /		
You /		ask.
We /		
They /	didn't	
He /		
She /		see.
It		

Wh- questions

	do	Subject	Verb
		I /	
		you /	ask?
		we /	
What	did	they /	
		he /	
		she /	see?
		it	

Yes / No questions

do	Subject	Verb
	I /	
	you /	
	we /	ask?
Did	they /	
	he /	see?
	she /	
	it	

Positive short answers

	Subject	*do*
	I /	
	you /	
	we /	
Yes,	they /	did.
	he /	
	she /	
	it	

Negative short answers

	Subject	*do*
	I /	
	you /	
	we /	
No,	they /	didn't.
	he /	
	she /	
	it	

Irregular verb (*be*)

Positive

Subject		
I / He / She / It	was	in London.
You / We / They	were	

Negative

Subject		
I / He / She / It	wasn't	in London.
You / We / They	weren't	

Wh- questions

		Subject
Where	was	I / he / she / it?
	were	you / we / they?

Yes / No questions

	Subject	
Was	I / he / she / it	in London?
Were	you / we / they	

Positive short answers

	Subject	
Yes,	I / he / she / it	was.
	you / we / they	were.

Negative short answers

	Subject	
No,	I / he / she / it	wasn't.
	you / we / they	weren't.

Form

Spelling: regular verbs in positive sentences
If the verb ends in a consonant, add -ed:

work → worked, play → played
• If the verb ends in -e, add -d:
arrive → arrived, decide → decided
• If the verb ends in a consonant + -y,
change -y to -i and add -ed:
marry → married, study → studied
• One-syllable verbs with a vowel
+ a final consonant, double the consonant
and add -ed:
stop → stopped, rob → robbed

Spelling: irregular verbs in positive sentences
See the Irregular verb list on page 143.

Use

Things which started and finished in the past
I saw Dominic yesterday and I talked to him for five minutes.

With time expressions

		yesterday.	
		yesterday morning / afternoon / evening.	
		last night / Sunday / week / month / year.	
		a year / two days / three weeks / four months **ago**.	
I went to the pub	**at**	9 o'clock.	(time)
		the weekend.	
		Christmas.	
I was in London	**on**	Saturday.	(day)
		28th August.	(date)
	in	July.	(month)
		the summer.	(season)
		1999.	(year)
		the morning.	(part of day)

Word search

Use the clues and circle the verbs and time expressions in
the puzzle (across and down).

Clues

1 **A:** Where were you at the weekend? (4)
2 **B:** I .... in St Ives with my boyfriend. (3)
3 She .... George a year ago, but divorced
   him six months later. (7)
4 They .... to a party last night. (4)
5 Did you .... in a hotel in Greece? (4)
6 I always go skiing .... the winter. (2)
7 I met him seven years .... (3)
8 The train arrived 9:15. (2)
9 I .... the book, but I didn't like the film. (5)
10 It's Sunday today, so .... was Saturday. (9)
11 They .... 1,000 people to their party. (7)
12 **A:** Who .... the match? (3)
    B: England did, 2–1.
13 I stayed in and .... TV last night. (7)
14 I was thirsty, so I .... a glass of water. (3)
15 When he .... the door, he saw the smoke. (6)
16 He didn't .... lunch. He wasn't hungry. (4)
17 What did he .... ? I couldn't hear. (3)
18 He flew to Turkey .... Sunday 3rd February. (2)

W	X	Y	Y	Z	A	G	O	A	L
O	W	E	N	T	B	C	D	E	I
N	A	S	F	L	D	U	V	I	K
C	S	T	A	Y	S	H	K	E	E
B	N	E	I	N	V	I	T	E	D
M	A	R	R	I	E	D	Q	W	R
T	Y	D	U	I	I	W	Y	J	O
D	W	A	T	C	H	E	D	B	P
S	A	Y	V	B	N	R	J	K	E
I	N	F	E	L	O	E	H	O	N
V	T	S	H	N	A	H	A	V	E
J	U	F	T	N	S	X	H	A	D
J	R	D	B	A	T	L	I	N	V

The future: Present Continuous and *'ll (will)* + verb (Unit 10)

Present Continuous

Form

See page 104 for the form of the Present Continuous.

Use

Definite future arrangements

We're going to the theatre on Friday.

(We decided to go to the theatre and we booked our tickets.)

'll (will) + verb

Positive

Subject		Verb
I / You / We / They /	'll	go.
He / She / It	(will)	play.

Negative

Subject		Verb
I / You / We / They /	won't	go.
He / She / It	(will not)	play.

Positive short answers

	Subject	
Yes,	I / you / we / they /	will.
	he / she / it	

Negative short answers

	Subject	
No,	I / you / we / they /	won't.
	he / she / it	

Form

Short answers don't use *'ll*

A: Are you going to Tom's party?

B: I don't know. Maybe I **will**.

A: I talked to Val. She's going.

B: Oh really. Maybe I **won't**.

Use

Future arrangements which aren't definite

A: What are you doing tonight?

B: I'm not sure. **Maybe I'll go** to the cinema – or **perhaps I'll stay** at home and watch a video. What about you? (B doesn't have a definite arrangement.)

A: Oh, I'm having a drink with some friends. (A has a definite arrangement.)

Crossword puzzle

Clues

ACROSS

1 Perhaps I .... go out tonight. I'm tired. (4)

3 .... they leaving Rome on 20th August? (3)

4 He's .... football next weekend. (7)

6 I'm .... for the football team tomorrow. Will you try too? (6)

7 A: Are you coming with us? B: I don't know. .... I will. (5)

8 I'm .... an old school friend at the weekend. (6)

12 We're .... a friend at the airport tomorrow. (7)

DOWN

1 A: Are you playing golf tomorrow? B: I don't know. Maybe I ....(4)

2 I'm .... my brother to the station after lunch. (6)

4 A: Are you coming? B: I'm not sure. .... I'll just go home. (7)

5 It's Al's birthday next Friday. His father's .... him a car! (6)

9 A: Is he arriving on Monday? B: No, he .... (4)

10 When are you .... to France? (5)

11 A: Are you taking the train to Moscow? B: .... , I am. (3)

Comparative adjectives (Unit 12)

Form

+ -er

For short adjectives (one syllable):

clean → cleaner, cheap → cheaper

But add -r for short adjectives (one syllable) ending in -e:

nice → nicer, late → later

Double consonant at the end + -er

For short adjectives with a vowel and a consonant at the end:

big → bigger, fat → fatter

-y → -i + -er

For two-syllable adjectives with -y at the end:

friendly → friendlier, easy → easier

more + adjective

Use more + adjective for long adjectives (most two-, three-, and four-syllable adjectives):

crowded → more crowded, comfortable → more comfortable

Irregular adjectives

good → better, bad → worse

than

We only use than with an object:

Trains (subject) are more comfortable **than** buses (object).

Use

Comparing

A: I like the Abbey Restaurant more. It's cheaper than the Garden Restaurant and the menu's nicer.

B: I prefer the Garden Restaurant. The people are friendlier and the food's better than the food at the Abbey Restaurant. The garden is more beautiful too!

Comparative adjectives or *not as* + adjective + *as*

We can compare things in different ways.

The red swimsuit **is cheaper than** the blue swimsuit.

The red swimsuit **isn't as expensive as** the blue swimsuit.

Crossword puzzle

Clues

ACROSS

1 There were a lot of people on the train. It was .... (7)

2 Sam got an A. Pat got a B. Sam's exam result is .... than Pat's. (6)

6 The opposite of *cheap*. (9)

7 The opposite of *smaller*. (6)

10 Anita's hair is very short. It's .... than her brother's hair. (7)

12 Scotland isn't as big .... England. (2)

13 The opposite of *early*. (4)

14 He's .... as nice as his wife. He never says "hello", but she's lovely. (3)

DOWN

1 It's .... to go by coach. The train costs more. (7)

3 English is .... to learn than Chinese. (6)

4 I love the food in that restaurant. It's .... (9)

5 The opposite of *ugly*. (9)

8 A gold watch is .... expensive than a plastic watch. (4)

9 Ted got a D. Eve got an E. Eve's exam result is .... than Ted's. (5)

11 Andy is 23 years old. Brian is 22. Andy is older .... Brian. (4)

12 She arrived home from the party .... 3 a.m. (2)

Present Perfect (Unit 13)

Positive

Subject	*have*	Past participle
I / You / We / They	've (have)	worked.
He / She / It	's (has)	driven.

Negative

Subject	*have*	Past participle
I / You / We / They	haven't (have not)	worked.
He / She / It	hasn't (has not)	driven.

Wh- questions

	have	Subject	Past participle
Where	have	I / you / we / they	worked?
	has	he / she /it	driven?

Yes / No questions

have	Subject	Past participle
Have	I / you / we / they	worked?
Has	he / she / it	driven?

Positive short answers

	Subject	*have*
Yes,	I / you / we / they	have.
	he / she / it	has.

Negative short answers

	Subject	*have*
No,	I / you / we / they	haven't.
	he / she / it	hasn't.

Form

Spelling: past participle (regular verbs)

The spelling and pronunciation (/d/, /t/ or /ɪd/) of the past participle are the same as the Past Simple.

Verb	Past Simple	Past participle
work	worked	worked

Spelling: past participle (irregular verbs)

Sometimes the past participle and the Past Simple are the same, sometimes different.

Verb	Past Simple	Past participle
have	had	had
see	saw	seen

Use

General past experience

I've travelled a lot.

Compare the Present Perfect and the Past Simple:

PRESENT PERFECT (general past experience)
A: **Have you ever been** to India?
B: Yes, **I have.**

PAST SIMPLE (details about the experience)
A: Oh? When **did you go**?
B: **I went** last year.

With *ever* = in your whole life

Have you **ever** met a famous person?

Been or gone?

Look at the difference:

I've **been** to France.

(I'm not in France now. I'm here.)

She's **gone** to France.

(She's in France now – at this moment.)

Secret adjective!

Find the secret adjective.

Clues

1 *Have / has* + past participle = the Present ....
2 He works for Ferrari and he's .... a lot of racing cars.
3 They've .... Mount Everest.
4 A: Where's Anthony? B: He's .... to work.
5 .... he been to Italy?
6 I've .... over 2,000 holiday photographs in my life!
7 What countries .... you been to?
8 She's .... her arm skiing three times.
9 I've .... in many different countries because of my work.
10 Have you ever .... to Trinidad?
11 They've .... a lot of money to poor people in their lives.

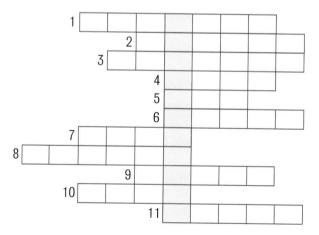

Want to do and *be going to do* (Unit 16)

Want to do

Positive

Subject		Verb
I / You / We / They	want to	go.
He / She / It	wants to	

Negative

Subject	*do*		Verb
I / You / We / They	don't	want to	go.
He / She / It	doesn't		

Wh- questions

	do	Subject		Verb
Why	do	I / you / we / they	want to	go?
	does	he / she / it		

Yes / *No* questions

do	Subject		Verb
Do	I / you / we / they	want to	go?
Does	he / she / it		

Positive short answers

	Subject	*do*
Yes,	I / you / we / they	do.
	he / she / it	does.

Negative short answers

	Subject	*do*
No,	I / you / we / they	don't.
	he / she / it	doesn't.

Form

Spelling

Want only changes to *wants* in positive sentences with *he, she, it*:
I want to go to France but he wants to go to Spain.

Use

Future dreams and ambitions

I want to change my life.

Be going to do

Positive

Subject	*be*		Verb
I	'm (am)	going to	go.
You /We / They	're (are)		
He / She / It	's (is)		

Negative

Subject	*be*		Verb
I	'm not (am not)	going to	go.
You / We / They	aren't (are not)		
He / She / It	isn't (is not)		

Wh- questions

	be	Subject		Verb
Where	am	I	going to	go?
	are	you /we / they		
	's (is)	he / she / it		

Yes / *No* questions

be	Subject		Verb
Am	I	going to	go?
Are	you / we / they		
Is	he / she / it		

Positive short answers

	Subject	*be*
Yes,	I	am.
	you / we / they	are.
	he / she / it	is.

Negative short answers

	Subject	*be*
No,	I	'm not.
	you / we / they	aren't.
	he / she / it	isn't.

Use

Future intentions and plans

I'm going to stay at home tonight and watch a video.

Compare *be going to do* and the Present Continuous:

BE GOING TO DO
(future intentions and plans)
A: I'm going to meet my brother.

PRESENT CONTINUOUS
(definite future arrangements)
B: I'm meeting my brother next Thursday.

But for future intention and plans with *go* and *come* we usually use the Present Continuous:
I'm going to Spain next year. **NOT** I'm go~~ing to go~~ to Spain next year.

Wavelength Crossword puzzle

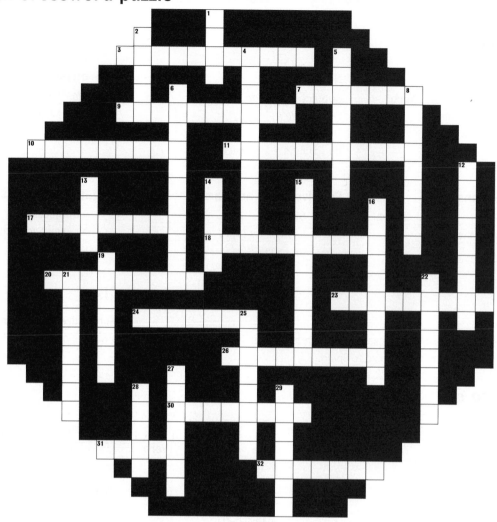

ACROSS

3   If you're .... , you're relaxed and warm. (11) (Unit 5)
7   If you're .... , you feel angry and unhappy because someone has something you want. (7) (Unit 3)
9   We use an .... to wake up in the morning. (5 / 5) (Unit 10)
10   The holiday two people take after they get married. (9) (Unit 12)
11   An .... person understands ideas and thinks quickly. (11) (Unit 12)
17   The first meal of the day. (9) (Unit 11)
18   A good-looking man or woman is .... (10) (Unit 9)
20   Earrings, necklaces, rings are all .... (9) (Unit 7)
23   Someone you work with is a .... (9) (Unit 2)
24   I was late for work this morning, the .... was terrible. (7) (Unit 8)
26   A big van to take people to hospital. (9) (Unit 15)
30   He wants to be a doctor. That's his .... (8) (Unit 16)
31   Not a child. (5) (Unit 1)
32   An expensive jewel. It doesn't usually have a colour. (7) (Unit 7)

DOWN

1   It sings and it flies in the sky. (4) (Unit 14)
2   Near to where you live. (5) (Unit 6)
4   I'm meeting my bank manager this afternoon. I've got an .... at two o'clock. (11) (Unit 10)
5   At the top of a newspaper article there is usually a .... (8) (Unit 6)
6   Your mother's mother is your .... (11) (Unit 13)
8   If you go brown in the sun, you're .... (9) (Unit 9)
12   If something is .... , it's fantastic. (9) (Unit 4)
13   A spoken or written test. (4) (Unit 15)
14   If you do this you feel calm and comfortable. (5) (Unit 3)
15   He has a very .... business. It makes a lot of money. (10) (Unit 4)
16   If you don't have a job, you're .... (10) (Unit 1)
19   He isn't in. Would you like to leave a .... (7) (Unit 2)
21   He's my boss. I'm his .... (8) (Unit 8)
22   Dream but not at night. (8) (Unit 16)
25   I send e-mails on my .... (8) (Unit 5)
27   The first part of a meal. (7) (Unit 13)
28   A white or grey thing in the sky. (5) (Unit 14)
29   Someone who travels for pleasure. (7) (Unit 11)

Key to Grammar reference puzzles

Be (Welcome pages: A and B)

Secret place!

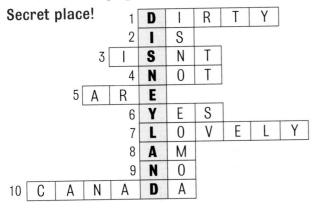

1. D I R T Y
2. I S
3. I S N T
4. N O T
5. A R E
6. Y E S
7. L O V E L Y
8. A M
9. N O
10. C A N A D A

The secret word is **DISNEYLAND**.

Present Simple (Units 1 and 2)

Secret job!

1. W A T C H E S
2. D O E S
3. S M O K E S
4. S P E A K
5. Y O U
6. G E T S
7. T H E Y
8. N E V E R

9. P L A Y
10. H A R D L Y
11. D O E S N T
12. G O E S
13. W R I T E S
14. A L W A Y S
15. S W I M S
16. M E E T S
17. E V E R
18. W H E R E

The secret job is **COMPUTER PROGRAMMER**.

Present Continuous (Unit 4)

Crossword puzzle

Have got / has got and have / has (Unit 5)

Pyramid puzzle

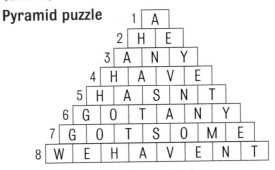

1. A
2. H E
3. A N Y
4. H A V E
5. H A S N T
6. G O T A N Y
7. G O T S O M E
8. W E H A V E N T

Past Simple (Units 6 and 7)

Word search

W	X	Y	Y	Z	A	G	O	A	L
O	W	E	N	T	B	C	D	E	I
N	A	S	F	L	D	U	V	I	K
C	S	T	A	Y	S	H	K	E	E
B	N	E	I	N	V	I	T	E	D
M	A	R	R	I	E	D	Q	W	R
T	Y	D	U	I	I	W	Y	J	O
D	W	A	T	C	H	E	D	B	P
S	A	Y	V	B	N	R	J	K	E
I	N	F	E	L	O	E	H	O	N
V	T	S	H	N	A	H	A	V	E
J	U	F	T	N	S	X	H	A	D
J	R	D	B	A	T	L	I	N	V

1 were		10 yesterday
2 was		11 invited
3 married		12 won
4 went		13 watched
5 stay		14 had
6 in		15 opened
7 ago		16 have
8 at		17 say
9 liked		18 on

The future: Present Continuous and 'll (will) + verb (Unit 10)
Crossword puzzle

Present Perfect (Unit 13)
Secret adjective!

The secret adjective is **FRIGHTENING**.

Comparative adjectives (Unit 12)
Crossword puzzle

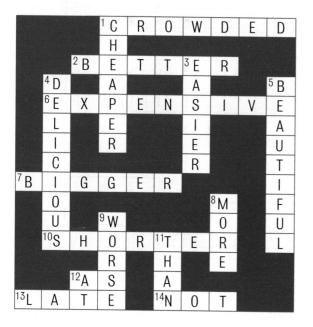

Want to do and be going to do (Unit 16)
Wavelength crossword puzzle

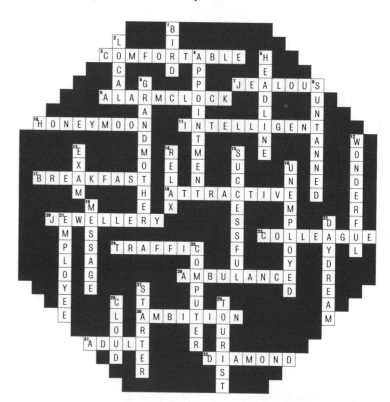

Information for pair and group work

Welcome D, Exercise 3, page 12

STUDENTS A AND B

The suitcases from Chaos Air flight 206 are missing. Each person or couple has lost four things. Match the people to their things. Then make sentences about them. Use *this, these, that, those.*

Examples: a) This is his suitcase.

          c) Those are their photographs.

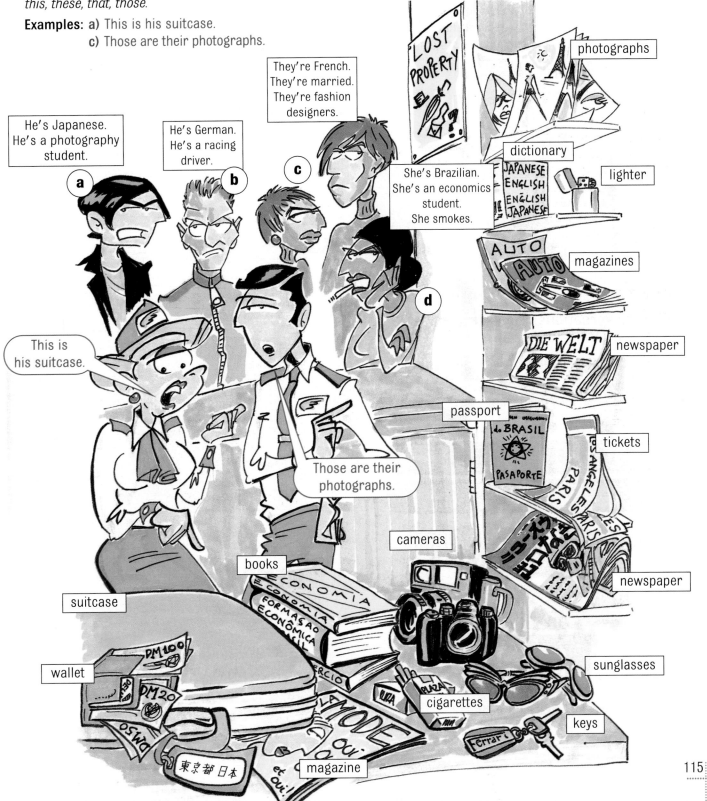

Unit 7 Skills, Exercise 2c), page 51

STUDENT A PART 1

• Read this information. Tell the other students in your group about it but don't show them. Then work together to fill in the Motives table on page 128.

This is Lord Pimm's friend, John Woodson. He visited Hadley Hall before the murder. The police interviewed him about the murder. Read the beginning of his police statement.

Police Statement No. 728

John Woodson   Date 18th May 1938

Lord Pimm and I are old friends. We went to school together. He invited me to stay for the weekend. I left four days before the murder. On Saturday I saw the butler and the gardener in the garden. They had an argument about money. They were both very angry. I heard the gardener say, "I gave you that money in December! It's May now! I want it back!" I didn't want them to see me so I . . .

• When you finish, look at Part 2, page 117.

Unit 2 Conversations, Exercise 4, page 23

STUDENT A PART 1

• Show Student B these signs. Ask questions about them. You begin.

Example: A: What does this mean?
              B: No smoking.

1 QUEUE HERE →

2 EXIT

3 The Pink Palace Hotel
   NO VACANCIES

4 ARRIVALS

5 push

• When you finish, look at Part 2, page 118.

Unit 7, Exercise 10, page 50

STUDENT A

Each of you went to one of the cities in the Word Box. You went to London. Take it in turns to ask and answer Yes/No questions and find out which city each student went to.

Moscow ✓ New York   London   Paris   Rome   Geneva
Tokyo   São Paulo   Barcelona   Hollywood

Example: A: Was it hot?   B: No, it wasn't.
              C: Did you eat caviar?   B: Yes, I did.
              D: Did you go to Moscow? B: Yes, I did.

Unit 12 *Do you remember?* 9–12, Exercise 3b), page 78

STUDENT A

Read your information. Then take it in turns to ask and answer the questions you wrote in Exercise 3a) on page 78.

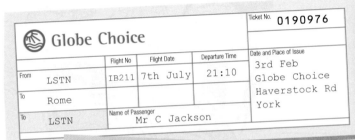

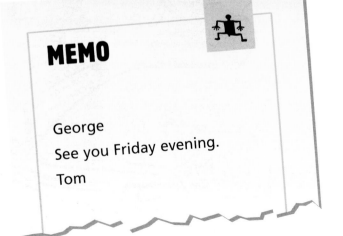

Unit 12 *Do you remember?* 9–12, Exercise 2, page 78

STUDENT A

Look at the picture below. Take it in turns to ask and answer questions to find six things in your shopping trolleys that are the same.

Example: Is / Are there any . . . ?
No, there isn't / aren't. OR Yes, there is / are.

Welcome C, Exercise 6, page 11

STUDENT A PART 1

• You begin. Show Student B Pictures 1, 2 and 3 and ask the names of the people. Fill in the gaps.

Examples: What's his / her name?
How do you spell that?

• When you finish, look at Part 2, page 119.

1 2 3

.... and ....

Unit 2 Conversations, Exercise 2c), page 23

STUDENT A

Have two conversations similar to Exercise 1a) on page 23.

a) You're the receptionist at the Metropole Hotel. The address is 118 Park Lane. You begin.

b) You're a business person. Phone the Queen's Hotel. Use your real name. Student B begins.

Unit 8 *Do you remember?* 5–8, Exercise 4, page 56

STUDENT A

You begin. Remember! You can't speak! Mime these things to the hotel receptionists.

• The bar is very crowded. Can I have a bottle of champagne and two glasses in my room (Room 13)?
• I left my wallet on the bus. I can't pay the bill.

Unit 7 Skills, Exercise 2c), page 51

STUDENT A PART 2

• Read the end of John Woodson's police statement from 18th May, look at the picture and read the card. Tell the other students in your group about the information but don't show them. Then work together to fill in the Motives table on page 128.

> . . . Lord Pimm and I had a long talk on Sunday morning. £10,000 was missing from their bank account. He wanted me to find out what Lady Pimm bought with the money. I went to Lady Pimm's favourite jeweller's when I got back to London. He told me that she spent £5,000 on a man's gold watch on 1st May. Lord Pimm was very sad when I told him. He loves that woman and the watch wasn't a present for him.

Freddie
A gold watch for my darling Freddie! I love you for ever. Matilda xx

• When you finish, look at Part 3, page 125.

Unit 7 Skills, Exercise 2c), page 51

STUDENT B PART 1

• Read this letter. Tell the other students in your group about it but don't show them. Then work together to fill in the Motives table on page 128.

> *Darling Tom,*
> *   Meet you in the garden at nine o'clock tonight. Please be careful. Don't tell Jenny! I love you, I love you, I love you,*
> *   Ruth X*

• When you finish, look at Part 2, page 119.

Unit 2 Conversations, Exercise 4, page 23

STUDENT A PART 2

Answer Student B's questions about these signs. Tell or act out the meaning.

6  This is the American word for toilets. You see this in public places like airports and restaurants.

7  You go in this door.

8  These are the times the planes or trains leave.

9  Use your hands to make the door move towards you.

10  The café isn't open. You can't eat there now.

Unit 7, Exercise 10, page 50

STUDENT B

Each of you went to one of the cities in the Word Box. You went to Paris. Take it in turns to ask and answer *Yes / No* questions and find out which city each student went to.

> Moscow ✓ New York London Paris Rome Geneva
> Tokyo São Paulo Barcelona Hollywood

Example:
B: Was it hot?	A: No, it wasn't.
C: Did you eat caviar?	A: Yes, I did.
D: Did you go to Moscow?	A: Yes, I did.

Unit 12 *Do you remember?* 9–12, Exercise 3b), page 78

STUDENT B

Read your information. Then take it in turns to ask and answer the questions you wrote in Exercise 3a) on page 78.

> Charles
> Remember your driving lesson on Tuesday afternoon.
> Mum

> Arts Theatre Cambridge
> **MACBETH**
> 23rd April
> 7.30 p.m.
> £15.00
> AT C
>
> Ms S Smith
> 36 Hill Street
> Bramerton
> NR14 7EQ
>
> (Price includes Booking Fee)
>
> To be retained
> Registered Charity No 123654
> VAT No 0987654321

> **TARGET BANKING**
>
> Dear Ms Thompson
> Account number: 5370659
>
> This is to confirm your meeting with the manager on 5th May.

Unit 12 *Do you remember?* 9–12, Exercise 2, page 78

STUDENT B
Look at the picture below. Take it in turns to ask and answer questions to find six things in your shopping trolleys that are the same.

Example: Is / Are there any . . . ?
No, there isn't / aren't. OR Yes, there is / are.

Welcome C, Exercise 6, page 11

STUDENT A PART 2
Look at Student B's pictures and answer the questions.

4	5	6
Mavis and Simon	Richard	Jenny

Unit 8 *Do you remember?* 5–8, Exercise 4, page 56

STUDENT B
You go second. Remember! You can't speak! Mime these things to the hotel receptionists.

• There's a fire in Room 10! Phone the emergency services now!
• The man from Room 20 rode his motorbike into the swimming pool!

Unit 16, Exercise 9, page 99

STUDENT C
You have these two problems. Take it in turns to talk about what you want to do and what you're going to do.

• You borrowed your friend's white jacket. You had an accident and spilled some red wine on it.
• You're watching a film in the cinema. A couple behind you are talking and making a lot of noise.

Unit 7 Skills, Exercise 2c), page 51

STUDENT B PART 2
• Read this information. Tell the other students in your group about it but don't show them. Then work together to fill in the Motives table on page 128.

• When you finish, look at Part 3, page 127.

Unit 7 Skills, Exercise 2c), page 51

STUDENT C PART 1

- Read this information. Tell the other students in your group about it but don't show them. Then work together to fill in the Motives table on page 128.

Dear Elsie,

Thank you so much for your letter. I'm very sad. We have terrible money problems. Tom played cards again last week and lost £100 – and he borrowed £1,000 from Freddie, the gardener last December. Now Freddie wants the money back and we don't have it! Freddie is horrible to Tom – and to his wife, Ruth. She had a black eye three days ago! Freddie says he loves me. He wants me to leave Tom and go away with him, but I hate him! Sometimes I want to kill him. And I love my Tom. I don't know what to do. Please write soon!

With love from,
Jenny

- When you finish, look at Part 2, page 121.

Unit 4 *Do you remember?* 1–4, Exercise 3b), page 34

STUDENT C

a) Read this to your group.

William loves going out but he hates crowded nightclubs. He usually goes to restaurants or quiet bars. He often goes to a museum or to an art gallery on Sunday afternoon. He likes spending time alone or with one or two friends.

b) When you finish, go back to Exercise 3c) on page 34.

Unit 2 Conversations, Exercise 4, page 23

STUDENT B PART 1

- Answer Student A's questions about these signs. Tell or act out the meaning.

Example: A: What does this mean?
          B: No smoking.

1

Stand in a line and wait.

2 **EXIT**

You go out of this door.

3 The Pink Palace Hotel — NO VACANCIES

All the rooms in the hotel are full.

4 **ARRIVALS**

These are the times the planes or trains come in to the airport.

5 **push**

Make the door open by using your hands.

- When you finish, look at Part 2, page 122.

Welcome C, Exercise 6, page 11

STUDENT B PART 1

- Look at Student A's pictures and answer the questions.

1   2   3

Carol and Marcus   Emily   Peter

- When you finish, look at part 2, page 123.

Unit 12 *Do you remember?* 9–12, Exercise 3b), page 78

STUDENT C

Read your information. Then take it in turns to ask and answer the questions you wrote in Exercise 3a) on page 78.

You are invited to the wedding of Charles Jackson and Susan Jones

Miss S J Smith
36 Hill Street
Bramerton

Jane,
Good Luck in your Italian test on Thursday.
Dad

━━━ Memo ━━━

```
To:     George
From:   Andy
Date:   2nd March

George,

See you at the golf course on
Wednesday afternoon.

Andy
```

Unit 1, Exercise 5, page 16

STUDENT A

a) You work for Vision Design. Student B wants a job as an accountant. Ask him / her the questions from Exercise 4b) on page 16. You begin.

b) Now swap. You want a job as a translator at Vision Design. Answer Student B's questions. Here is your information.

your company?	GTM International
job?	translator
languages?	Arabic, Spanish, English and Portuguese
study?	yes – Japanese / Law
want this job?	very good company / like hard work
free time?	listen to music

Unit 7, Exercise 10, page 50

STUDENT C

Each of you went to one of the cities in the Word Box. You went to Hollywood. Take it in turns to ask and answer *Yes / No* questions and find out which city each student went to.

> Moscow ✓ New York   London   Paris   Rome   Geneva
> Tokyo   São Paulo   Paris   Barcelona   Hollywood

Example: A: Was it hot?   B: No, it wasn't.
c: Did you eat caviar?   B: Yes, I did.
D: Did you go to Moscow?   B: Yes, I did.

Unit 8 *Do you remember?* 5–8, Exercise 4, page 56

STUDENT C

You go third. Remember! You can't speak! Mime these things to the hotel receptionists.

- A beautiful young woman got into my car and drove it away! Phone the police now!
- I left my computer in the gym yesterday. It isn't there now. Is it here?

Unit 7 Skills, Exercise 2c), page 51

STUDENT C PART 2

- Read this letter. Tell the other students in your group about it but don't show them. Then work together to fill in the Motives table on page 128.

My darling Freddie
Why do you love Jenny and not me?!
She doesn't have any money.
She's only a cook. She can't buy you things,
but I can. Don't be a fool.
You know that I love you!
All my love
Matilda

- When you finish, look at Part 3, page 122.

Unit 7, Exercise 10, page 50

STUDENT D

Each of you went to one of the cities in the Word Box. You went to Rome. Take it in turns to ask and answer *Yes / No* questions and find out which city each student went to.

> Moscow✓ New York London Paris Rome Geneva
> Tokyo São Paulo Barcelona Hollywood

Example:
- A: Was it hot?
- C: Did you eat caviar?
- D: Did you go to Moscow?
- B: No, it wasn't.
- B: Yes, I did.
- B: Yes, I did.

Unit 12 *Do you remember?* 9–12, Exercise 3b), page 78

STUDENT D

Read your information. Then take it in turns to ask and answer the questions you wrote in Exercise 3a) on page 78.

View of Tower Bridge

Sal
See you at Victoria Station at 2 o'clock on Saturday.
Sue

Sally Smith
36 Hill St.
Bramerton

Elizabeth postcards - views of the

Skyline Holidays

Name of passenger

Miss Jane Thompson

From	Departure date
LHR	12th June
To Buenos Aires	Departure time 20:50

Flight No

BA191

ONE WAY

MEMO

Tom
Do you want to come with us to Barcelona this weekend? We're going by car!
George

Unit 2 Conversations, Exercise 4, page 23

STUDENT B PART 2

Show Student A these signs. Ask questions about them. You begin.

6 **Restrooms**

7 **ENTRANCE**

8 **DEPARTURES**

9 **PULL**

10 **CLOSED**

Unit 7 Skills, Exercise 2c), page 51

STUDENT C PART 3

- Read this police statement. Tell the other students in your group about it but don't show them. Then work together to fill in the Time and place table on page 128.

Police Statement   No. 729

Tom Wiggit, the butler   Date 19th May 1938

I work in the dining room from 7:00 to 8:00 every evening with Ruth, the maid. I went to Lord Pimm's room at 8:00 and we played cards. I lost £10. Lord Pimm's OK, but I don't like his wife. She was always with Freddie, the gardener. At 8:30 I went to Freddie and Ruth's room because he wanted to see me. He wasn't there. I waited for about thirty minutes but he didn't come. At 9:00 I went to the garden for a cigarette. I saw Freddie but he was busy and he didn't speak to me. I also saw Ruth, the maid and we had a conversation. We saw Lord Pimm in the garden. At about 10:00 we went back to the house. I had a cup of tea with Jenny and Ruth in the kitchen. Lady Pimm called for Ruth and then we heard the shot.

- When you finish, go back to Exercise 3 on page 51.

Unit 16, Exercise 9, page 99

STUDENT D

You have these two problems. Take it in turns to talk about what you want to do and what you're going to do.

- A private clinic has asked you to take a new drug as an experiment. They are going to pay you. The drug is very new and they want to see if it is dangerous.
- At your job interview you said you spoke perfect English. Next week an English diplomat is coming to your company. He doesn't speak your language.

Unit 4 *Do you remember?* 1–4, Exercise 3b), page 34

STUDENT D

a) Read this to your group.

Luke is a very active, healthy person. He loves doing sports and being outdoors. He lives in the city but he doesn't like it because it's so crowded. He often goes to the country at the weekend.

b) When you finish, go back to Exercise 3c) on page 34.

Unit 8, Exercise 9, page 55

STUDENTS A AND B

Take it in turns to apologise and react.

APOLOGISE

I'm really sorry.
(Tell him / her the problem)
The car broke down again and . . .
The buses were terrible . . .
(Give more details)
So, I tried to stop a taxi but . . .
So, I walked to . . .
(Use adjectives)
It was awful! Terrible!

REACT

Are you angry?
But you're always late!
Well, thanks a lot!

Are you sympathetic?
Oh, no. Oh . . . poor you!
Don't worry. It's OK.

Unit 1, Exercise 5, page 16

STUDENT B

a) You want a job as an accountant at Vision Design. Answer Student A's questions. Here is your information.

your company?	PTS International
job?	accountant
languages?	French, Italian, English and Japanese
study?	yes – Economics / Spanish
want this job?	interesting / big company
free time?	visit friends

b) Now swap. You work for Vision Design. Student A wants a job as a translator. Ask him / her the questions from Exercise 4b) on page 16.

Unit 2 Conversations, Exercise 2c), page 23

STUDENT B

Have two conversations similar to Exercise 1a) on page 23.

a) You're a business person. Phone the Metropole Hotel. Use your real name. Student A begins.

b) You're the receptionist at the Queen's Hotel. The address is 28 Brompton Road. You begin.

Welcome C, Exercise 6, page 11

STUDENT B PART 2

Show Student A Pictures 4, 5 and 6 and ask the names of the people. Fill in the gaps.

Examples: What's his / her name?
How do you spell that?

4   5   6

.... and ....

Welcome B, Exercise 3, page 9

STUDENT A

a) You begin. Use the questions from Exercise 1a) on page 8. Ask Student B about Silvia and George and fill in the table.

b) Answer Student B's questions about Marta and Barry.

name?	Marta	Barry	Silvia	George
country?	Poland	The USA		
married?	single	divorced		
nice?	lovely	awful		

Unit 9, Exercise 6b), page 61

STUDENTS A, B, C AND D

a) You have an idea for a film. Talk about these questions and fill in the table.

1 What type of film is it? A love story / an action film / a horror film / a comedy / a musical?
2 Where does the film happen? In Italy / a house in the mountains?
3 When does it happen? In the future / in the 1950s / now?
4 What are the names of the hero, heroine and villain?
5 What are they like? Selfish / shy? What do they look like? Tall / ugly?
6 Do they work? What do they do? What do they do in their free time?
7 What actors / actresses do you want for the parts? Why?
8 What is the title of the film?

The film			
Title?			
Type?			
Where?			
When?			
The parts	Name	Description	Actor / actress
The hero			
The heroine			
The villain			
A short description of the story			

b) When you finish, go back to Exercise 6c) on page 61.

Unit 16, Exercise 9, page 99

STUDENT A
You have these two problems. Take it in turns to talk about what you want to do and what you're going to do. You begin.

- You've arranged to babysit for a friend's baby this evening. A person you like very much phones and asks you to go out with him / her.
- You look at your bank statement. The bank has put a lot of money into your bank account by mistake.

Unit 4 *Do you remember?* 1–4, Exercise 2, page 34

STUDENT A

a) Read about Barbara.

Barbara is from San Francisco in the United States. She lives in London. Her boyfriend, Steve, is an accountant and Barbara is a teacher. She walks to work because she doesn't have a car. In her free time Barbara loves playing tennis. She's very healthy and she doesn't smoke. She loves listening to classical music but Steve hates classical music so she listens to it on her own. She likes travelling and wants to learn French because she doesn't speak any foreign languages. When she wants to relax she reads magazines and listens to classical music.

b) Ask Student B questions about Charlotte and answer questions about Barbara. Find five things they have in common and five differences.

Example: A: Where does Charlotte live?
B: She lives in London.
A: Oh, they both live in London.

Unit 7 Skills, Exercise 2c), page 51

STUDENT A PART 3

• Read these police statements. Tell the other students in your group about them but don't show them. Then work together to fill in the Time and place table on page 128.

Police Statement   No. 730

Lord Pimm   Date 19th May 1938

My wife and I had dinner in the dining room. It was very good. She left at 8:00. She always goes for a walk after dinner. I went to my room. My butler was there. We played cards and he lost about £10. He left at about 8:30. Then I went to my wife's room. We had a conversation about a small money problem and I was angry. My wife doesn't like talking about money. I left her room at 9:00 and went to the garden. I was in the garden for about an hour. At about 10:00 I saw the cook go into the house. Lovely little thing. Then I went to my room. About five minutes later I heard the shot.

Police Statement   No. 731

Lady Pimm   Date 19th May 1938

I was in the dining room from 7:00 to 8:00. I had dinner with my husband, Lord Pimm. At about 8:00 I went for a walk in the garden. I always go for a walk after dinner. The garden is very beautiful in the evening. I saw the gardener. At about 8:30 I went to my room. I saw Jenny, the cook, go into the garden then. My husband came to my room and we had a conversation about a little problem. It wasn't important. He left at about 9:00. I went to bed but I didn't sleep. At 10:00 I called for my maid. She brought me a cup of tea. I heard the shot soon after. It was terrible.

• When you finish, go back to Exercise 3 on page 51.

Unit 4 *Do you remember?* 1–4, Exercise 3b), page 34

STUDENT A

a) You begin. Read this to your group.

Joshua is quite an active person. He doesn't stay at home very often. He really likes going out and having fun. He often goes to nightclubs with his friends, but he's also quite healthy and does a lot of different sports.

b) When you finish, go back to Exercise 3c) on page 34.

Unit 4 *Do you remember?* 1–4, Exercise 1, page 34

GROUP A

a) Look at these answers. Work together and write one question for each answer.

Example: Yes, I am. (answer)
Are you Spanish? / from Spain? / a woman? / a student? / a doctor? (possible questions)

1 No, I don't. 3 Yes, he does. 5 J-O-U-R-N-A-L-I-S-T
2 Polish.   4 Yes, always.   6 The USA.

b) Play the game. You begin. Tell Group B your first answer. If they give you a good question for your answer, they get one point. If their question is exactly the same as your question, they get two points!

c) Group B tells you their first answer. Continue with the game and take it in turns to tell each other your answers.

Unit 3 Day to day English, Exercise 4, page 29

ALL STUDENTS

a) Match the pictures to the words in the Word Box.

> coffee✓ cheese sandwich tea cigarette ham
> sandwich cigar beer orange juice red wine
> white wine whisky vodka and tonic

Example: a) = coffee

b) Go round the class. Take it in turns to offer people things from the Word Box and answer *Yes* or *No*.

Example: A: Would you like something to eat – a cheese sandwich?
B: Yes, please. That sounds nice. Would you like a cigarette?
A: No, thanks. I don't smoke.

Unit 3, Exercise 7b), page 27

STUDENTS A AND B

Check Bob's answers and fill in his score. Then do the same for your partner.

Are you a "people person" or a loner?

Do you . . .	love	really like	like	don't mind	don't like	hate
1 talking to friends?	6	5	4	3	1	0
2 going out with friends?	6	5	4	3	1	0
3 spending time alone?	0	1	2	3	5	6
4 meeting new people?	6	5	4	3	1	0
5 going on holiday alone?	0	2	2	2	1	0
6 going to parties?	6	5	4	3	1	0
7 staying at home?	0	1	2	2	3	5

Bob's score: ☐   My partner's score: ☐

0–14 You're a real loner. Maybe you don't like people very much. You really like spending time on your own. Spend more time with your family and friends and relax with them!

15–31 Maybe your social life isn't very busy, but it's fine for you and you have some good friends. Your friends are important to you and you like spending time with them. You like going out and meeting new people sometimes, but you also like staying in and having quiet evenings, maybe alone.

32–42 You really like people and they really like you. You have a busy social life and often go out with friends or telephone them because you don't like spending time on your own. This is OK, but learn to enjoy time alone as well.

Do you look after yourself?

Do you . . .	love	really like	like	don't mind	don't like	hate
1 doing sports?	6	5	4	3	1	0
2 going for walks?	6	5	4	3	1	0
3 watching TV?	0	2	3	4	6	0
4 active holidays?	6	5	4	3	1	0
5 relaxing on holiday?	0	1	2	3	5	6
6 healthy food?	6	5	4	3	1	0
7 smoking?	0	1	2	3	5	6

Bob's score: ☐   My partner's score: ☐

0–14 You're not a very active person! You love sleeping, watching TV and sitting around. You're a very relaxed person but you aren't very healthy. Enjoy yourself but be careful about your health too. Don't smoke so many cigarettes. Eat some healthy food – it's not dangerous! Go for a walk sometimes.

15–31 You've got a good lifestyle. You like exercise and doing things but you often relax too. You're relaxed and healthy.

32–42 Help! You're a really active person and you have a lot of interests but you're probably not a very relaxed person. In fact you hardly ever relax! Learn to enjoy the little pleasures in life – watch TV or listen to some quiet music.

Unit 16, Exercise 9, page 99

STUDENT B

You have these two problems. Take it in turns to talk about what you want to do and what you're going to do.

• You saw your friend's boyfriend on holiday with another woman. You are meeting your friend this evening.

• A good friend is going into hospital for a serious operation. You have an important interview on the same day.

Unit 4 *Do you remember?* 1–4, Exercise 2, page 34

STUDENT B

a) Read about Charlotte.

Charlotte is from London. She's a lawyer and her boyfriend, Jasper, is an accountant with a large company. She lives near Piccadilly Circus in London. Charlotte has a small car and at the weekends they often visit their friends, who live by the sea. In the evening she usually watches TV, reads magazines or listens to classical music because she works hard in the day. She hates exercise. She sometimes plays tennis with Jasper but she hates it because he always wins. She smokes a lot. Every summer she goes to Spain on holiday but she doesn't speak Spanish. She only speaks English.

b) Ask Student A questions about Barbara and answer questions about Charlotte. Find five things they have in common and five differences.

Example: B: Where does Barbara live?
   A: She lives in London.
   B: Oh, they both live in London.

Unit 7 Skills, Exercise 2c), page 51

STUDENT B PART 3

• Read these two police statements. Tell the other students in your group about them but don't show them. Then work together to fill in the Time and place table on page 128.

Police Statement   No. 732

Jenny Wiggit, the cook   Date 19th May 1938

I was in the kitchen from 6:00 to about 8:30. I gave the gardener his dinner. He left the kitchen at 8:00. I think he went to the garden. I went for a walk in the garden at about 8:30. I saw the gardener again. Just before 10:00 I went back to the house. Ruth and Tom, my husband, were in the kitchen. Lady Pimm called for Ruth. Then we heard the shot.

Police Statement   No. 733

Ruth Kettle, the maid   Date 19th May 1938

Lord and Lady Pimm have dinner at 7:00 so the butler, Tom, and I are always in the dining room from 7:00 to 8:00. Yesterday was the same. At 8:00 I had my dinner in the kitchen with Jenny, the cook. We left at about 8:30. I went to the garden. It's lovely there. At about 9:00 I saw the gardener. Then at about 9:30 I saw the butler, we talked for a few minutes. We went back to the house just before 10:00. We went to the kitchen and made some tea. Then Jenny came in. At about 10:00 Lady Pimm called. I took her a cup of tea and then we heard the shot. Now my Freddie's dead . . .

• When you finish, go back to Exercise 3 on page 51.

Unit 4 *Do you remember?* 1–4, Exercise 1, page 34

GROUP B

a) Look at these answers. Work together and write one question for each answer.

Example: Yes, I am. (answer)
    Are you Spanish? / from Spain? / a woman? /
    a student? / a doctor? (possible questions)

1 Italy.   3 No, never.   5 No, he doesn't.
2 Yes, I do.   4 S-E-C-R-E-T-A-R-Y   6 Japanese.

b) Play the game. Group A tells you their first answer. If you give them a good question for their answer, you get one point. If your question is exactly the same as their question, you get two points!

c) Tell Group A your first answer. Continue with the game and take it in turns to tell each other your answers.

Unit 4 *Do you remember?* 1–4, Exercise 3b), page 34

STUDENT B

a) Read this to your group.

Ben is a "people person". He really likes going out with his friends. He doesn't really like spending time alone. He loves sport but he's a bit lazy so he just watches it on TV, usually with his friends.

b) When you finish, go back to Exercise 3c) on page 34.

Unit 5 Day to day English, Exercise 4, page 40

STUDENTS A AND B

In pairs. Look at the pictures. What are the people saying? Use the words in the Word Box and have conversations.

use / comb   take / car   join / you

Example: A: Can . . .
                B: Well, . . .

Unit 7 Skills, Exercise 2b), page 51

MOTIVES TABLE

Lord Cedric Pimm	Jealous: his wife loved Freddie.
Lady Matilda Pimm	
Tom Wiggit, the butler	
Jenny Wiggit, the cook	
Ruth Kettle, the maid	

TIME AND PLACE TABLE

	7:00–8:00	8:00–8:30	8:30–9:00	9:00–10:00	10:00–10:30
Lord Cedric Pimm	dining room				
Lady Matilda Pimm					
Tom Wiggit, the butler					
Jenny Wiggit, the cook					
Freddie Kettle, the gardener					
Ruth Kettle, the maid					

Welcome B, Exercise 3, page 9

STUDENT B

a) Answer Student A's questions about Silvia and George.

b) Use the questions from Exercise 1a) on page 8. Ask Student B about Marta and Barry and fill in the table.

name?	Silvia	George	Marta	Barry
country?	Germany	Canada		
married?	single	married		
nice?	OK	all right		

Word lists

A list of useful words from each unit (n = noun, v = verb, adj = adjective, adv = adverb, det = determiner, prep = preposition, pron = pronoun)

Welcome A

COUNTRY	NATIONALITY	LANGUAGE	COUNTRY	NATIONALITY	LANGUAGE
Argentina	Argentinian	Spanish	Italy	Italian	Italian
Australia	Australian	English	Japan	Japanese	Japanese
Belgium	Belgian	Flemish/French	Korea	Korean	Korean
Brazil	Brazilian	Portuguese	Mexico	Mexican	Spanish
Bulgaria	Bulgarian	Bulgarian	Poland	Polish	Polish
Chile	Chilean	Spanish	Portugal	Portuguese	Portuguese
China	Chinese	Chinese	Russia	Russian	Russian
The Czech Republic	Czech	Czech	Scotland	Scottish	English/Gaelic
Ecuador	Ecuadorian	Spanish	Slovakia	Slovak	Slovak
Egypt	Egyptian	Arabic	Spain	Spanish	Spanish
England	English	English	Taiwan	Taiwanese	Chinese
France	French	French	Turkey	Turkish	Turkish
Germany	German	German	The United Kingdom	British	English
Greece	Greek	Greek	Uruguay	Uruguayan	Spanish
Hungary	Hungarian	Hungarian	The USA	American	English
Ireland	Irish	English/Gaelic	Wales	Welsh	English/Welsh

again (adv) /əˈgen, əˈgeɪn/
all (det) /ɔːl/
always (adv) /ˈɔːlwɪz, -weɪz/
answer (v) /ˈɑːnsə/
business (n) /ˈbɪznɪs/
child/children (n) /tʃaɪld, ˈtʃɪldrən/
from (prep) /frəm, frɒm/
help (n and v) /help/
how (adv) /haʊ/
important (adj) /ɪmˈpɔːtənt/

in (prep) /ɪn/
listen [to] (v) /ˈlɪsən/
look [at] (v) /lʊk/
meet (v) /miːt/
nice (adj) /naɪs/
often (adv) /ˈɒfən, ˈɒftən/
on (prep) /ɒn/
photograph (n) /ˈfəʊtəgrɑːf/
read (v) /riːd/
say (v) /seɪ/

[the] sea (n) /siː/
shop (n) /ʃɒp/
then (conj) /ðen/
to (prep) /tə, tʊ/
where (adv) /weə/
which (det) /wɪtʃ/
word (n) /wɜːd/
write (v) /raɪt/

Welcome B

PERSONAL PRONOUNS

subject	object
I /aɪ/	me /miː/
you /jʊ, juː/	you /jʊ, juː/
we /wiː/	us /əs, ʌs/
they /ðeɪ/	them /ðem/
he /hiː/	him /hɪm/
she /ʃiː/	her /hɜː/
it /ɪt/	it /ɪt/

add (v) /æd/
all right (adj) /ɔːl ˈraɪt/
any (det) /ˈeni/
awful (adj) /ˈɔːfəl/
bank (n) /bæŋk/
beach (n) /biːtʃ/
beautiful (adj) /ˈbjuːtɪfəl/
before (prep) /brɪˈfɔː/
boring (adj) /ˈbɔːrɪŋ/
change (v) /tʃeɪndʒ/
clean (adj) /kliːn/

conversation (n) /kɒnvəˈseɪʃən/
dirty (adj) /ˈdɜːti/
divorced (adj) /dɪˈvɔːst/
expensive (adj) /ɪkˈspensɪv/
good (adj) /gʊd/
find (v) /faɪnd/
friendly (adj) /ˈfrendli/
horrible (adj) /ˈhɒrɪbəl/
hotel (n) /həʊˈtel/
interesting (adj) /ˈɪntrɪstɪŋ/
kilometre (n) /ˈkɪləmiːtə/
lovely (adj) /ˈlʌvli/
man (n) /mæn/
married (adj) /ˈmærɪd/
museum (n) /mjuːˈziːəm/
near (prep) /nɪə/
nightclub (n) /ˈnaɪtklʌb/
or (conj) /ə, ɔː/
people (n) /ˈpiːpəl/
person (n) /ˈpɜːsən/

place (n) /pleɪs/
pool (n) /puːl/
postcard (n) /ˈpəʊstkɑːd/
really (adv) /ˈrɪəli/
restaurant (n) /ˈrestərɒnt/
road (n) /rəʊd/
shop (n) /ʃɒp/
single (adj) /ˈsɪŋgəl/
some (det) /səm, sʌm/
student (n) /ˈstjuːdənt/
table (n) /ˈteɪbəl/
too (adv) /tuː/
unfriendly (adj) /ʌnˈfrendli/
use (v) /juːz/
who (pron) /huː/
wife (n) /waɪf/
with (prep) /wɪð, wɪθ/
woman (n) /ˈwʊmən/
writer (n) /ˈraɪtə/

Welcome C

NUMBERS

1	one /wʌn/	first /fɜːst/
2	two /tuː/	second /ˈsekənd/
3	three /θriː/	third /θɜːd/
4	four /fɔː/	fourth /fɔːθ/
5	five /faɪv/	fifth /fɪfθ, fɪftθ/
6	six /sɪks/	sixth /sɪksθ/
7	seven /ˈsevən/	seventh /ˈsevənθ/
8	eight /eɪt/	eighth /eɪtθ/
9	nine /naɪn/	ninth /naɪnθ/
10	ten /ten/	tenth /tenθ/

POSSESSIVE ADJECTIVES

my /maɪ/
your /jə, jɔː/
our /aʊə/
their /ðeə/
his /hɪz/
hers /hɜː/
its /ɪts/

address (n) /əˈdres/
alphabet (n) /ˈælfəbet/
book (n) /bʊk/
check in/into (v) /tʃek ˈɪn, ˈɪntə/
drink (n) /drɪŋk/
floor (n) /flɔː/
form (n) /fɔːm/
ground floor (n) /graʊnd ˈflɔː/
guest (n) /gest/
information (n) /ɪnfəˈmeɪʃən/

letter (n) /ˈletə/
Miss /mɪs/
Mr /ˈmɪstə/
Mrs /ˈmɪsɪz/
Ms /mɪz/
name (n) /neɪm/
notebook (n) /ˈnəʊtbʊk/
partner (n) /ˈpɑːtnə/
picture (n) /ˈpɪktʃə/
reception (n) /rɪˈsepʃən/

receptionist (n) /rɪˈsepʃənɪst/
[on the] right (adj) /raɪt/
room (n) /ruːm, rʊm/
spell (v) /spel/
spelling (n) /ˈspelɪŋ/
surname (n) /ˈsɜːneɪm/
that (det) /ðæt/
toilet (n) /ˈtɔɪlɪt/

Welcome D

NUMBERS

11	eleven /ɪˈlevan/	40	forty /ˈfɔːti	101	a / one hundred and one /ə hʌndrɪd ən ˈwʌn/
12	twelve /twelv/	43	forty-three /fɔːti ˈθriː/	200	two hundred /tuː ˈhʌndrɪd/
13	thirteen /θɜːˈtiːn/	50	fifty /ˈfɪfti/	1,000	a / one thousand /ə ˈθaʊzənd/
14	fourteen /fɔːˈtiːn/	54	fifty-four /fɪfti ˈfɔː/	1,009	a / one thousand and nine /ə ˈθaʊzənd ən ˈnaɪn/
15	fifteen /fɪfˈtiːn/	60	sixty /ˈsɪksti/		
16	sixteen /sɪkˈstiːn/	65	sixty-five /sɪksti ˈfaɪv/	1,215	one thousand, two hundred and fifteen /wʌn ˈθaʊzənd tuː ˈhʌndrɪd ən ˈfɪftiːn/
17	seventeen /sevənˈtiːn/	70	seventy /ˈsevənti/		
18	eighteen /eɪˈtiːn/	76	seventy-six /sevənti ˈsɪks/		
19	nineteen /naɪnˈtiːn/	80	eighty /ˈeɪti/	100,000	a / one hundred thousand /ə ˈhʌndrɪd ˈθaʊzənd/
20	twenty /ˈtwenti/	87	eighty-seven /eɪti ˈsevən/		
21	twenty-one /twenti ˈwʌn/	90	ninety /ˈnaɪnti/	1,000,000	a / one million /ə ˈmɪljən/
30	thirty /ˈθɜːti/	98	ninety-eight /naɪnti ˈeɪt/		
32	thirty-two /θɜːti ˈtuː/	100	a / one hundred /ə ˈhʌndrɪd/		

about (adv) /əˈbaʊt/
bag (n) /bæg/
[bank] account (n) /əˈkaʊnt/
battery (n) /ˈbætəri/
briefcase (n) /ˈbriːfkeɪs/
camera (n) /ˈkæmərə/
cassette (n) /kəˈset/
cigar (n) /sɪˈgɑː/
cigarette (n) /sɪgəˈret/
classroom (n) /ˈklɑːsruːm/
clock (n) /klɒk/
designer (n) /dɪˈzaɪnə/
dictionary (n) /ˈdɪkʃənəri/
dollar ($) (n) /ˈdɒlə/
economics (n) /ekəˈnɒmɪks/
excuse (v) /ɪkˈskjuːz/

fashion (n) /ˈfæʃən/
half (n) /hɑːf/
key (n) /kiː/
know (v) /nəʊ/
lighter (n) /ˈlaɪtə/
magazine (n) /mægəˈziːn/
[mobile] phone (n) /məʊbaɪl ˈfəʊn/
money (n) /ˈmʌni/
newspaper (n) /ˈnjuːspeɪpə/
orange (n) /ˈɒrəndʒ/
passport (n) /ˈpɑːspɔːt/
past (prep) /pɑːst/
personal stereo (n) /pɜːsənəl ˈsteriəʊ/
photography (n) /fəˈtɒgrəfi/
please (v) /pliːz/
population (n) /pɒpjuˈleɪʃən/
pound (£) (n) /paʊnd/

quarter (n) /ˈkwɔːtə/
racing driver (n) /ˈreɪsɪŋ draɪvə/
sell (v) /sel/
smoke (v) /sməʊk/
suitcase (n) /ˈsuːtkeɪs/
sunglasses (n, pl) /ˈsʌnglɑːsɪz/
thank you /ˈθæŋk juː/
these (det) /ðiːz/
thing (n) /θɪŋ/
think (v) /θɪŋk/
this (det) /ðɪs/
those (det) /ðəʊz/
ticket (n) /ˈtɪkɪt/
time (n) /taɪm/
today (n) /təˈdeɪ/
wallet (n) /ˈwɒlɪt/
watch (n) /wɒtʃ/

Unit 1 All work and no play

above (prep) /əˈbʌv/
abroad (n) /əˈbrɔːd/
accountant (n) /əˈkaʊntənt/
activity (n) /ækˈtɪvɪti/
adult (n) /ˈædʌlt/
advertisement (n) /ədˈvɜːtɪsmənt/
afternoon (n) /ɑːftəˈnuːn/
answer (n) /ˈɑːnsə/
artist (n) /ˈɑːtɪst/
at (prep) /ət, æt/
ball (n) /bɔːl/
[the] ballet (n) /ˈbæleɪ/
bank (n) /bæŋk/
bar (n) /bɑː/
basketball (n) /ˈbɑːskɪtbɔːl/
because (conj) /bɪˈkɒz/
bed (n) /bed/
beginner (n) /bɪˈgɪnə/
bicycle (n) /ˈbaɪsɪkəl/
boss (n) /bɒs/
break (n) /breɪk/
bring (v) /brɪŋ/
brochure (n) /ˈbrəʊʃə/
busy (adj) /ˈbɪzi/
[the] cinema (n) /ˈsɪnəmə/
city (n) /ˈsɪti/
choose (v) /tʃuːz/
class (n) /klɑːs/
coffee (n) /ˈkɒfi/
college (n) /ˈkɒlɪdʒ/
company (n) /ˈkʌmpəni/
court (n) /kɔːt/
creative (adj) /kriˈeɪtɪv/
cycling (n) /ˈsaɪklɪŋ/

DAYS OF THE WEEK

Monday /ˈmʌndi/
Tuesday /ˈtjuːzdi/
Wednesday /ˈwenzdi/
Thursday /ˈθɜːzdi/
Friday /ˈfraɪdi/
Saturday /ˈsætədi/
Sunday /ˈsʌndi/

department (n) /dɪˈpɑːtmənt/
design (n) /dɪˈzaɪn/
do (v) /duː/
doctor (n) /ˈdɒktə/
engineer (n) /endʒɪˈnɪə/
enjoy (v) /ɪnˈdʒɔɪ/
equipment (n) /ɪˈkwɪpmənt/
evening (n) /ˈiːvnɪŋ/
every (adj) /ˈevri/
experienced (adj) /ɪkˈspɪəriənst/
expert (n) /ˈekspɜːt/
family (n) /ˈfæməli/

fishing (n) /ˈfɪʃɪŋ/
fit (adj) /fɪt/
flight attendant (n) /ˈflaɪt ətendənt/
football (n) /ˈfʊtbɔːl/
for (prep) /fɔːr, fə/
free (adj) /friː/
friend (n) /frend/
[in] front [of] (prep) /frʌnt/
fun (n) /fʌn/
get up (v) /get ˈʌp/
go (v) /gəʊ/
golf (n) /gɒlf/
gym (n) /dʒɪm/
hard (adv) /hɑːd/
hard-working (adj) /ˈhɑːd ˈwɜːkɪŋ/
holiday (n) /ˈhɒlɪdi/
[at] home (n) /həʊm/
horse-riding (n) /ˈhɔːs raɪdɪŋ/
house (n) /haʊs/
individual (adj) /ɪndɪˈvɪdʒuəl/
indoor (adj) /ˈɪndɔː/
international (adj) /ɪntəˈnæʃənəl/
interview (n) /ˈɪntəvjuː/
job (n) /dʒɒb/
join (v) /dʒɔɪn/
journalist (n) /ˈdʒɜːnəl-ɪst/
Latin America (n) /ˈlætɪn əˈmerɪkə/
lawyer (n) /ˈlɔːjə/
learn (v) /lɜːn/
leave (v) /liːv/
leisure (n) /ˈleʒə/
leisure centre (n) /ˈleʒə ˈsentə/
lesson (n) /ˈlesən/
level (n) /ˈlevəl/
like (v) /laɪk/
lunch (n) /lʌntʃ/
keep (v) /kiːp/
make (v) /meɪk/
management (n) /ˈmænɪdʒmənt/
manager (n) /ˈmænɪdʒə/
meeting (n) /ˈmiːtɪŋ/
modern (adj) /ˈmɒdən/
[at the] moment (n) /ˈməʊmənt/
month (n) /mʌnθ/
morning (n) /ˈmɔːnɪŋ/
music (n) /ˈmjuːzɪk/
musician (n) /mjuːˈzɪʃən/
need (v) /niːd/
night (n) /naɪt/
nothing (pron) /ˈnʌθɪŋ/
office (n) /ˈɒfɪs/
old (adj) /əʊld/
only (adv) /ˈəʊnli/
open (adj) /ˈəʊpən/
other (adj) /ˈʌðə/

[the] opera (n) /ˈɒpərə/
out (prep) /aʊt/
outdoor (adj) /ˈaʊtdɔː/
part (n) /pɑːt/
personal (adj) /ˈpɜːsənəl/
play (n and v) /pleɪ/
player (n) /ˈpleɪə/
price (n) /praɪs/
professional (n) /prəˈfeʃənəl/
programme (n) /ˈprəʊgræm/
pub (n) /pʌb/
question (n) /ˈkwestʃən/
quickly (adv) /ˈkwɪkli/
racket (n) /ˈrækɪt/
relax (v) /rɪˈlæks/
relaxed (adj) /rɪˈlækst/
report (n) /rɪˈpɔːt/
round (adv) /raʊnd/
run (v) /rʌn/
sales (n) /seɪlz/
secretary (n) /ˈsekrətəri/
see (v) /siː/
short (adj) /ʃɔːt/
sit (v) /sɪt/
skiing (n) /ˈskiːɪŋ/
small (adj) /smɔːl/
so (conj) /səʊ/
sometimes (adv) /ˈsʌmtaɪmz/
speak (v) /spiːk/
study (n and v) /ˈstʌdi/
swap (v) /swɒp/
swim (v) /swɪm/
swimming (n) /ˈswɪmɪŋ/
talk (v) /tɔːk/
teacher (n) /ˈtiːtʃə/
team (n) /tiːm/
[tele-]phone (n and v) /ˈtelɪfəʊn/
television / TV (n) /ˈtelɪvɪʒən, tiːˈviː/
tennis (n) /ˈtenɪs/
[the] theatre (n) /ˈθɪətə/
tired (adj) /taɪəd/
town (n) /taʊn/
trainers (n) /ˈtreɪnəz/
translator (n) /trænsˈleɪtə/
trip (n) /trɪp/
true (adj) /truː/
under (prep) /ˈʌndə/
unemployed (adj) /ʌnɪmˈplɔɪd/
university (n) /juːnɪˈvɜːsɪti/
usually (adv) /ˈjuːʒuəli/
video game (n) /ˈvɪdiəʊ geɪm/
volleyball (n) /ˈvɒlibɔːl/
waiter / waitress (n) /ˈweɪtə, ˈweɪtrɪs/
wake up (v) /ˈweɪk ˈʌp/
want (v) /wɒnt/

wear (v) /weə/
weekend (n) /wi:k'end/
work (n and v) /wɜ:k/
year (n) /jɪə, jɜ:/
yoga (n) / 'jəʊgə/

Unit 2 Family, friends and neighbours

after (conj) / 'ɑ:ftə/
airport (n) / 'eəpɔ:t/
angry (adj) / 'æŋgri/
argue (v) / 'ɑ:gju:/
arrivals (n, pl) /ə'raɪvəlz/
arrive (v) /ə'raɪv/
begin (v) /bɪ'gɪn/
beginning (n) /bɪ'gɪnɪŋ/
boyfriend (n) / 'bɔɪfrend/
brother (n) / 'brʌðə/
businessman (n) / 'bɪznɪsmən/
business person (n) / 'bɪznɪs pɜ:sən/
businesswoman (n) / 'bɪznɪswʊmən/
classmate (n) / 'klɑ:smeɪt/
closed (adj) /kləʊzd/
colleague (n) / 'kɒli:g/
dad (n) /dæd/
daughter (n) / 'dɔ:tə/
departures (n) /dɪ'pɑ:tʃəz/
different (adj) / 'dɪfərənt/
dinner (n) /dɪnə/
downstairs (adv) /daʊn'steəz/
early (adj) / 'ɜ:li/
entrance (n) / 'entrəns/
everywhere (adv) / 'evriweə/
except (prep) /ɪk'sept/
exit (n) / 'egzɪt/
family (n) / 'fæməli/
fast (adj) /fɑ:st/
father (n) /fɑ:ðə/
flat (n) /flæt/
girlfriend (n) / 'gɜ:lfrend/
give (v) /gɪv/
glad (adj) /glæd/
great (adj) /greɪt/
guitar (n) /gɪ'tɑ:/
happy (adj) / 'hæpi/
hardly ever (adv) / 'hɑ:dli 'evə/
hate (v) /heɪt/
hour (n) /aʊə/
hurry (n and v) / 'hʌri/
husband (n) / 'hʌzbənd/
invite (v) /ɪn'vaɪt/
late (adj) /leɪt/
letter (n) / 'letə//
life (n) /laɪf/
line (n) /laɪn/
live (v) /lɪv/

long (adj) /lɒŋ/
[a] lot [of] (n) /lɒt/
love (v) /lʌv/
lunchtime (n) / 'lʌntʃtaɪm/
mean (v) /mi:n/
medicine (n) / 'medsən/
message (n) / 'mesɪdʒ/
mum (n) /mʌm/
neighbour (n) / 'neɪbə/
never (adv) / 'nevə/
new (adj) /nju:/
next door (adv) /nekst 'dɔ:/
now (adv) /naʊ/
often (adv) / 'ɒfən/
parent (n) / 'peərənt/
piano (n) /pi'ænəʊ/
polite (adj) /pə'laɪt/
problem (n) / 'prɒbləm/
put (v) /pʊt/
queue (v and n) /kju:/
real (adj) /rɪəl/
reservation (n) /rezə'veɪʃən/
restroom (n) / 'restru:m/
rude (adj) /ru:d/
rush (v) /rʌʃ/
sister (n) / 'sɪstə/
slowly (adv) / 'sləʊli/
smile (v) /smaɪl/
smoking (n) / 'sməʊkɪŋ/
son (n) /sʌn/
sorry (adj) / 'sɒri/
stay (v) /steɪ/
stop (v) /stɒp/
strange (adj) /streɪndʒ/
street (n) /stri:t/
take (v) /teɪk/
take time off (v) /teɪk 'taɪm 'ɒf/
teach (v) /ti:tʃ/
terrible (adj) / 'terɪbəl/
thanks (n) /θæŋks//
tonight (n) /tə'naɪt/
towards (prep) /tə'wɔ:dz/
upstairs (adv) / 'ʌp'steəz/
vacancy (n) / 'veɪkənsi/
when (adv) /wen/
wife (n) /waɪf/

Unit 3 Lifestyles

active (adj) / 'æktɪv/
alone (adj) /ə'ləʊn/
beer (n) /bɪə/
café (n) / 'kæfeɪ/
can / can't (v) /kæn, kɑ:nt/
careful (adj) / 'keəfəl/
cheese (n) /tʃi:z/
clever (adj) / 'klevə/

concert (n) / 'kɒnsət/
cup (n) /kʌp/
dangerous (adj) / 'deɪndʒərəs/
don't / doesn't mind (v) /dəʊnt, dʌzənt 'maɪnd/
eat (v) /i:t/
fantastic (adj) /fæn'tæstɪk/
fine (adj) /faɪn/
fly (v) /flaɪ/
food (n) /fu:d/
glass (n) /glɑ:s/
go out [with] (v) /gəʊ 'aʊt/
ham (n) /hæm/
healthy (adj) / 'helθi/
hungry (adj) / 'hʌŋgri/
interest (n) / 'ɪntrɪst/
interested [in] (adj) / 'ɪntrɪstɪd/
jealous (adj) / 'dʒeləs/
journey (n) / 'dʒɜ:ni/
kind [of] (n) /kaɪnd/
lie (v) /laɪ/
lifestyle (n) / 'laɪfstaɪl/
loner (n) / 'ləʊnə/
look after (v) / 'lʊk 'ɑ:ftə/
maybe (adv) / 'meɪbi/
nervous (adj) / 'nɜ:vəs/
offer (n and v) / 'ɒfə/
on [your] own /ɒn [jʊə] 'əʊn/
orange juice (n) / 'ɒrəndʒ 'dʒu:s/
paint (v) /peɪnt/
painting (n) / 'peɪntɪŋ/
partner (n) / 'pɑ:tnə/
party (n) / 'pɑ:ti/
plane (n) /pleɪn/
probably (adv) / 'prɒbəbli/
questionnaire (n) /kwestʃə'neə/
quiet (adj) / 'kwaɪət/
rain (v and n) /reɪn/
red (adj) /red/
relax (v) /rɪ'læks/
relaxing (adj) /rɪ'læksɪŋ/
sandwich (n) / 'sænwɪdʒ/
score (v) /skɔ:/
shopping (n) / 'ʃɒpɪŋ/
sing (v) /sɪŋ/
snack (n) /snæk/
social (adj) / 'səʊʃəl/
sound (v) /saʊnd/
spend (v) /spend/
sport (n) /spɔ:t/
sunshine (n) / 'sʌnʃaɪn/
tea (n) /ti:/
thirsty (adj) / 'θɜ:sti/
tonic (n) / 'tɒnɪk/
violin (n) /vaɪə'lɪn/
vodka (n) / 'vɒdkə/

warm (adj) /wɔːm/
weather (n) /weðə/
walk (v and n) /wɔːk/
well (adv) /wel/
whisky (n) / ˈwɪski/
white (adj) /waɪt/
wine (n) /waɪn/
yourself (pron) /jəˈself/

Unit 4 Secrets and lies

art gallery (n) / ˈɑːt gæləri/
baby (n) / ˈbeɪbi/
babysitter (n) / ˈbeɪbiˌsɪtə/
bill (n) /bɪl/
both (det) /bəʊθ/
boyfriend (n) /ˈbɔɪfrend/
[good] bye /baɪ/
classical music (n) / ˈklæsɪkəl ˈmjuːzɪk/
crowded (adj) / ˈkraʊdɪd/
fight (v) /faɪt/
footballer (n) / ˈfʊtbɔːlə/
foreign (adj) / ˈfɒrən/
[the] future (n) / ˈfjuːtʃə/
gamble (v) / ˈgæmbəl/
habit (n) / ˈhæbɪt/
here (prep) /hɪə/
hold (v) /həʊld/
ice cream (n) / ˈaɪs ˈkriːm/
knife (n) /naɪf/
lie (n and v) /laɪ/
often (adv) / ˈɒftən/
[the] past (n) /pɑːst/
point (n and v) /pɔɪnt/
remember (v) /rɪˈmembə/
rob (v) /rɒb/
routine (n) /ruːˈtiːn/
shower (n) / ˈʃaʊə/
shine (v) /ʃaɪn /
spend time (v) /spend taɪm/
successful (adj) /səkˈsesfəl/
[the] truth (n) /truːθ/
wonderful (adj) / ˈwʌndəfəl/
worry [about] (v) / ˈwʌri/

Unit 5 You are what you wear

addict (n) / ˈædɪkt/
[go] ahead /əˈhed/
apple (n) / ˈæpəl/
beige (adj) /beɪʒ/
big (adj) /bɪg/
black (adj) /blæk/
blue (adj) /bluː/
boot (n) /buːt/
borrow (v) / ˈbɒrəʊ/
brown (adj) /braʊn/

car (n) /kɑː/
carry (v) / ˈkæri/
cash (n) /kæʃ/
cat (n) /kæt/
CD (n) / ˈsiː ˈdiː/
cheque (n) /tʃek/
chocolate (n) / ˈtʃɒklɪt/
clothes (n, pl) /kləʊz/
coat (n) /kəʊt/
cold (adj) /kəʊld/
colour (n) / ˈkʌlə/
comb (n) /kəʊm/
comfortable (adj) / ˈkʌmftəbəl/
computer (n) /kəmˈpjuːtə/
cotton (n) / ˈkɒtn/
credit card (n) / ˈkredɪt kɑːd/
dark (adj) /dɑːk/
darling (n) / ˈdɑːlɪŋ/
disco (n) / ˈdɪskəʊ/
dog (n) /dɒg/
door (n) /dɔː/
down (prep) /daʊn/
dress (n) /dres/
fashionable (adj) / ˈfæʃənəbəl/
green (adj) /griːn/
hat (n) /hæt/
hole (n) /həʊl/
honest (adj) / ˈɒnɪst/
jacket (n) / ˈdʒækɪt/
jeans (n, pl) /dʒiːnz/
jumper (n) / ˈdʒʌmpə/
label (n) / ˈleɪbəl/
large (adj) /lɑːdʒ/
laugh (v) /lɑːf/
light (adj) /laɪt/
light (n) /laɪt/
luck (n) /lʌk/
marry (v) / ˈmæri/
material (n) /məˈtɪəriəl/
maze (n) /meɪz/
medium (adj) / ˈmiːdiəm/
news (n) /njuːz/
open (v) / ˈəʊpən/
opinion (n) /əˈpɪnjən/
[a] pair of (n) / ˈpeər əv/
pay (v) /peɪ/
pen (n) /pen/
pink (adj) /pɪŋk/
plastic (adj) / ˈplæstɪk/
pyjamas (n, pl) /pəˈdʒɑːməz/
reason (n) / ˈriːzən/
refuse (v) /rɪˈfjuːz/
rich (adj) /rɪtʃ/
sandal (n) / ˈsændl/
school (n) /skuːl/
shirt (n) /ʃɜːt/
shoe (n) /ʃuː/

shop assistant (n) / ˈʃɒp əsɪstənt/
shorts (n, pl) /ʃɔːts/
shut (v) /ʃʌt/
silk (n) /sɪlk/
size (n) /saɪz/
skirt (n) /skɜːt/
slob (n) /slɒb/
sock (n) /sɒk/
someone (pron) / ˈsʌmwən/
smart (adj) /smɑːt/
suit (n) /suːt/
sure (adj) /ʃɔː/
sweatshirt (n) / ˈswet-ʃɜːt/
swimsuit (n) / ˈswɪmsuːt/
tie (n) /taɪ/
trainer (n) / ˈtreɪnə/
trousers (n, pl) / ˈtraʊzəz/
try (v) /traɪ/
T-shirt (n) / ˈtiː ʃɜːt/
turn down (v) / ˈtɜːn ˈdaʊn/
turn off (v) / ˈtɜːn ˈɒf/
turn on (v) / ˈtɜːn ˈɒn/
turn up (v) / ˈtɜːn ˈʌp/
victim (n) / ˈvɪktɪm/
way (n) /weɪ/
win (v) /wɪn/
window (n) / ˈwɪndəʊ/
wool (n) /wʊl/
wrong (adj) /rɒŋ/
yellow (adj) / ˈjeləʊ/

Unit 6 Have we got news for you!

actress (n) / ˈæktrɪs/
against (prep) /əˈgenst/
ago (adj) /əˈgəʊ/
arrest (v) /əˈrest/
article (n) / ˈɑːtɪkəl/
autograph (n) / ˈɔːtəgrɑːf/
back (adv) /bæk/
bottle (n) / ˈbɒtl/
boxer (n) / ˈbɒksə/
buy (v) /baɪ/
come (v) /kʌm/
couple (n) / ˈkʌpəl/
dancer (n) / ˈdɑːnsə/
destroy (v) /dɪˈstrɔɪ/
die (v) /daɪ/
diet cola (n) /daɪət ˈkəʊlə/
divorce (v) /dɪˈvɔːs/
emergency services (n, pl) /ɪˈmɜːdʒənsi ˈsɜːvɪsɪz/
escape (v) /ɪˈskeɪp/
everyone (pron) / ˈevriwʌn/
exciting (adj) /ɪkˈsaɪtɪŋ/
fan (n) /fæn/

133

favourite (adj) / ˈfeɪvərɪt/
film (n) /fɪlm/
fire (n) /faɪə/
forest (n) / ˈfɒrɪst/
freezer (n) / ˈfriːzə/
goal (n) /gəʊl/
happen (v) / ˈhæpən/
headline (n) / ˈhedlaɪn/
hospital (n) / ˈhɒspɪtl/
injure (v) / ˈɪndʒə/
invite (v) /ɪnˈvaɪt/
jump (v) /dʒʌmp/
kitchen (n) / ˈkɪtʃən/
last (adj) /lɑːst/
leg (n) /leg/
local (adj) / ˈləʊkəl/
luckily (adv) / ˈlʌkɪli/
madam (n) / ˈmædəm/
[football] match (n) /mætʃ/
meat (n) /miːt/
[the] media (n, pl) / ˈmiːdiə/
middle (n) / ˈmɪdl/
mistake (n) /mɪˈsteɪk/
news (n) /njuːz/
next door (adv) / ˈnekst ˈdɔː/
next [to] (prep) /nekst/
police (n) /pəˈliːs/
present (n) / ˈprezənt/
radio (n) / ˈreɪdiəʊ/
react (v) /riˈækt/
relationship (n) /rɪˈleɪʃənʃɪp/
score (v) /skɔː/
show (v) /ʃəʊ/
sir (n) /sɜː/
star (n) /stɑː/
start (v) /stɑːt/
story (n) / ˈstɔːri/
supermarket (n) / ˈsuːpəmɑːkɪt/
surprise (n and v) /səˈpraɪz/
taxi (n) / ˈtæksi/
teenage (adj) / ˈtiːneɪdʒ/
tree (n) /triː/
vegetarian (n and adj) /vedʒəˈteəriən/
victory (n) / ˈvɪktəri/
wedding (n) / ˈwedɪŋ/
yesterday (n) / ˈjestədi/

Unit 7 Round the world

almost (adv) / ˈɔːlməʊst/
amazing (adj) /əˈmeɪzɪŋ/
another (det) /əˈnʌðə/
area (n) / ˈeəriə/
argument (n) / ˈɑːgjʊmənt/
boat (n) /bəʊt/
butler (n) / ˈbʌtlə/
card (n) /kɑːd/
caviar (n) / ˈkæviɑː/

clear (adj) /klɪə/
cocktail (n) / ˈkɒkteɪl/
cook (n) /kʊk/
dead (adj) /ded/
dear (adj) /dɪə/
delicious (adj) /dɪˈlɪʃəs/
diamond (n) / ˈdaɪəmənd/
dining room (n) / ˈdaɪnɪŋ ruːm/
eye (n) /aɪ/
finally (adv) / ˈfaɪnəli/
find out (v) /faɪnd ˈaʊt/
fish (n) /fɪʃ/
fool (n) /fuːl/
fresh (adj) /freʃ/
fruit (n) /fruːt/
garden (n) / ˈgɑːdn/
gardener (n) / ˈgɑːdnə/
gold (adj) /gəʊld/
guide (n) /gaɪd/
hot (adj) /hɒt/
ill (adj) /ɪl/
jeweller's (n) / ˈdʒuːələz/
jewellery (n) / ˈdʒuːəlri/
kill (v) /kɪl/
lose (v) /luːz/
maid (n) /meɪd/

MONTHS OF THE YEAR

January / ˈdʒænjʊri/
February / ˈfebjʊri/
March / ˈmɑːtʃ/
April / ˈeɪprəl/
May /meɪ/
June /dʒuːn/
July /dʒʊˈlaɪ/
August / ˈɔːgəst/
September /sepˈtembə/
October /ɒkˈtəʊbə/
November /nəʊˈvembə/
December /dɪˈsembə/

mosquito (n) /məˈskiːtəʊ/
mountain (n) / ˈmaʊntɪn/
murder (n) / ˈmɜːdə/
noisy (adj) / ˈnɔɪzi/
politician (n) /pɒlɪˈtɪʃən/
pop (n) /pɒp/
queen (n) /kwiːn/
reason (n) / ˈriːzən/
send (v) /send/
shoot (v) /ʃuːt/
shot (n) /ʃɒt/
shy (adj) /ʃaɪ/
singer (n) / ˈsɪŋə/
statement (n) / ˈsteɪtmənt/
steal (v) /stiːl/

stupid (adj) / ˈstjuːpɪd/
tell (v) /tel/
together (adv) /təˈgeðə/
travel (v) / ˈtrævəl/
triangle (n) / ˈtraɪæŋgəl/
tropical (adj) / ˈtrɒpɪkəl/
understand (v) /ʌndəˈstænd/
visit (v) / ˈvɪzɪt/
wait (v) /weɪt/
wet (adj) /wet/
world (n) /wɜːld/

Unit 8 Trains and boats and planes

accident (n) / ˈæksɪdənt/
apologise (v) /əˈpɒlədʒaɪz/
arm (n) /ɑːm/
beard (n) /bɪəd/
bench (n) /bentʃ/
bike (n) /baɪk/
break down (v) /breɪk ˈdaʊn/
briefcase (n) / ˈbriːfkeɪs/
bus (n) /bʌs/
call (n) /kɔːl/
catch (v) /kætʃ/
champagne (n) /ʃæmˈpeɪn/
Christmas (n) / ˈkrɪsməs/
cold (n) /kəʊld/
cost (v) /kɒst/
crash (v) /kræʃ/
crowded (adj) / ˈkraʊdɪd/
cycle (v) / ˈsaɪkəl/
drive (v) /draɪv/
employee (n) /emplɔɪˈiː/
excuse (n) /ɪkˈskjuːs/
female (adj) / ˈfiːmeɪl/
foot (n) /fʊt/
forget (v) /fəˈget/
get in / into / off / out of (v) /get ˈɪn,
    ˈɪntə, ˈɒf, ˈaʊt əv/
glasses (n) / ˈglɑːsɪz/
love-sick (adj) / ˈlʌv ˈsɪk/
meaning (n) / ˈmiːnɪŋ/
mime (v) /maɪm/
miss (v) /mɪs/
motorbike (n) / ˈməʊtəbaɪk/
part-time (adj) / ˈpɑːt ˈtaɪm/
pick up (v) / ˈpɪk ˈʌp/
platform (n) / ˈplætfɔːm/
police officer (n) /pəˈliːs ɒfɪsə/
professor (n) /prəˈfesə/
psychology (n) /saɪˈkɒlədʒi/
push (v) /pʊʃ/
ride (v) /raɪd/
run away (v) / ˈrʌn əˈweɪ/
seat (n) /siːt/

station (n) /'steɪʃən/
traffic (n) /'træfɪk/
train (n) /treɪn/
transport (n) /'trænspɔ:t/
[the] Tube (n) /tju:b/
type (n) /taɪp/
[the] Underground (n) /'ʌndəɡraʊnd/
wave (v) /weɪv/

Unit 9 He has personality and looks!

action film (n) /'ækʃən 'fɪlm/
actor (n) /'æktə/
agent (n) /'eɪdʒənt/
anywhere (adv) /'eniweə/
attractive (adj) /ə'træktɪv/
bald(-ing) (adj) /bɔ:ld, 'bɔ:ldɪŋ/
blonde (adj) /blɒnd/
care (v) /keə/
comedy (n) /'kɒmədi/
congratulations (n, pl) /kəngrætʃʊ'leɪʃənz/
cool (adj) /ku:l/
curly (adj) /'kɜ:li/
difficult (adj) /'dɪfɪkəlt/
driving test (n) /'draɪvɪŋ test/
ex-boyfriend / girlfriend (n) /'eks
   'bɔɪfrend, -'gɜ:lfrend/
fat (adj) /fæt/
filmscript (n) /'fɪlm,skrɪpt/
get married (v) /get 'mærɪd/
good-looking (adj) /'gʊd 'lʊkɪŋ/
grey (adj) /greɪ/
hair (n) /heə/
handsome (adj) /'hænsəm/
helpful (adj) /'helpfəl/
hero (n) /'hɪərəʊ/
heroine (n) /'herəʊɪn/
herself (pron) /hə'self/
horror film (n) /'hɒrə ,fɪlm/
iced (adj) /aɪst/
joke (n and v) /dʒəʊk/
lazy (adj) /'leɪzi/
[be] like (v) /laɪk/
look like (v) /'lʊk laɪk/
looks (n, pl) /lʊks/
loud (adj) /laʊd/
moustache (n) /mə'stɑ:ʃ/
musical (n) /'mju:zɪkəl/
part (n) /pɑ:t/
pass (v) /pɑ:s/
personality (n) /pɜ:sə'næləti/
president (n) /'prezɪdənt/
pretty (adj) /'prɪti/
private detective (n) /praɪvət dɪ'tektɪv/
rest (n) /rest/
scene (n) /si:n/

selfish (adj) /'selfɪʃ/
sexy (adj) /'seksi/
silly (adj) /'sɪli/
situation (n) /sɪtʃu'eɪʃən/
slim (adj) /slɪm/
sporty (adj) /'spɔ:ti/
stepmother (n) /'stepmʌðə/
suntanned (adj) /'sʌntænd/
sweet (adj) /swi:t/
tall (adj) /tɔ:l/
ugly (adj) /ʌgli/
villain (n) /'vɪlən/
wavy (adj) /'weɪvi/

Unit 10 What are you doing for the rest of your life?

alarm clock (n) /ə'lɑ:m klɒk/
appointment (n) /ə'pɔɪntmənt/
arrangement (n) /ə'reɪndʒmənt/
birthday (n) /'bɜ:θdeɪ/
calendar (n) /'kæləndə/
definite (adj) /'defɪnət/
diary (n) /'daɪəri/
e-mail (n) /'i: meɪl/
film première (n) /'fɪlm 'premɪeə/
full (adj) /fʊl/
funny (adj) /'fʌni/
invitation (n) /ɪnvɪ'teɪʃən/
jet-setter (n) /'dʒet 'setə/
let's / us (v) /lets, 'let əs/
organised (adj) /'ɔ:gənaɪzd/
perhaps (adv) /pə'hæps/
plan (v) /plæn/
reply (n and v) /rɪ'plaɪ/
shall/'ll /ʃəl, ʃæl, əl/
studio (n) /'stju:dɪəʊ/
suggest (v) /sə'dʒest/
suggestion (n) /sə'dʒestʃən/
will/'ll (v) /wɪl, əl/

Unit 11 What a mouthful!

anything (pron) /'eniθɪŋ/
apple (n) /'æpəl/
bacon (n) /'beɪkən/
beans (n, pl) /bi:nz/
beef (n) /bi:f/
biscuit (n) /'bɪskɪt/
bread (n) /bred/
break (n) /breɪk/
breakfast (n) /'brekfəst/
butter (n) /'bʌtə/
cabbage (n) /'kæbɪdʒ/
cake (n) /keɪk/
carrot (n) /'kærət/
carton (n) /'kɑ:tn/
cereal (n) /'sɪərɪəl/

chef (n) /ʃef/
chicken (n) /'tʃɪkən/
chips (n, pl) /tʃɪps/
crisps (n, pl) /krɪsps/
definitely (adv) /'defɪnətli/
desk (n) /desk/
egg (n) /eg/
especially (adv) /ɪ'speʃəli/
famous (adj) /'feɪməs/
fork (n) /fɔ:k/
fried (adj) /fraɪd/
garlic (n) /'gɑ:lɪk/
grape (n) /greɪp/
greasy (adj) /'gri:si/
hamburger (n) /'hæmbɜ:gə/
heart attack (n) /'hɑːt ə'tæk/
lamb [chop] (n) /læm/
lemon (n) /'lemən/
lettuce (n) /'letɪs/
marmalade (n) /'mɑ:məleɪd/
meal (n) /mi:l/
melon (n) /'melən/
milk (n) /mɪlk/
mineral water (n) /'mɪnərəl 'wɔ:tə/
mouthful (n) /'maʊθfəl/
mug (n) /mʌg/
mushroom (n) /'mʌʃru:m/
onion (n) /'ʌnjən/
pasta (n) /'pæstə/
pear (n) /peə/
perfect (adj) /'pɜ:fɪkt/
plate (n) /pleɪt/
pleasure (n) /'pleʒə/
pork [chop] (n) /pɔ:k/
possible (adj) /'pɒsɪbəl/
potato (n) /pə'teɪtəʊ/
prawn (n) /prɔ:n/
recommend (v) /rekə'mend/
rice (n) /raɪs/
ridiculous (adj) /rɪ'dɪkjʊləs/
same (adj or pron) /seɪm/
salad (n) /'sæləd/
sausage (n) /'sɒsɪdʒ/
serve (v) /sɜ:v/
slow (adj) /sləʊ/
soup (n) /su:p/
spoon (n) /spu:n/
steak (n) /steɪk/
strawberry (n) /'strɔ:bəri/
sugar (n) /'ʃʊgə/
tasteless (adj) /'teɪstlɪs/
tasty (adj) /'teɪsti/
toast (n) /təʊst/
tomato (n) /tə'mɑ:təʊ/
tourist (n) /'tʊərɪst/
vegetable (n) /'vedʒtəbəl/

water (n) / ˈwɔːtə/

Unit 12 It's bigger and better

believe (v) /bɪˈliːv/
building (n) /ˈbɪldɪŋ/
cheap (adj) /tʃiːp/
cheers! /tʃɪəz/
church (n) /tʃɜːtʃ/
close (v) /kləʊz/
confirm (v) /kənˈfɜːm/
cook (v) /kʊk/
corridor (n) / ˈkɒrɪdɔː/
cream (n) /kriːm/
course (n) /kɔːs/
design (v) /dɪˈzaɪn/
easy (adj) / ˈiːzi/
health (n) /helθ/
honeymoon (n) / ˈhʌnimuːn/
intelligent (adj) /ɪnˈtelɪdʒənt/
jar (n) /dʒɑː/
lift (n) /lɪft/
madness (n) / ˈmædnɪs/
market (n) / ˈmɑːkɪt/
more (adv) /mɔː/
opposite (prep) / ˈɒpəzɪt/
product (n) /ˈprɒdʌkt/
romantic (adj) /rəʊˈmæntɪk/
skin (n) /skɪn/
soft (adj) /sɒft/
test (n) /test/
than (conj) /ðən, ðæn/
trolley (n) / ˈtrɒli/

Unit 13 Life stories

across (prep) /əˈkrɒs/
adventure (n) /ədˈventʃə/
attack (v) /əˈtæk/
bite (v) /baɪt/
block (n) /blɒk/
brave (adj) /breɪv/
claustrophobia (n) /klɔːstrəˈfəʊbiə/
climb (v) /klaɪm/
climber (n) / ˈklaɪmə/
completely (adv) /kəmˈpliːtli/
confident (adj) / ˈkɒnfɪdənt/
cry (v) /kraɪ/
customer (n) / ˈkʌstəmə/
desert (n) / ˈdezət/
dessert (n) /dɪˈzɜːt/
engine (n) / ˈendʒɪn/
ever (adv) / ˈevə/
exactly (adv) /ɪgˈzæktli/
experience (n) /ɪkˈspɪəriəns/
farm (n) /fɑːm/

farmer (n) / ˈfɑːmə/
fear (n) /fɪə/
frightened [of] (adj) / ˈfraɪtnd/
frightening (adj) / ˈfraɪtn-ɪŋ/
grandmother (n) / ˈgrænmʌðə/
grilled (adj) /grɪld/
height (n) /haɪt/
lonely (adj) / ˈləʊnli/
main course (n) / ˈmeɪn ˈkɔːs/
menu (n) / ˈmenjuː/
nobody (pron) / ˈnəʊbədi/
order (v) / ˈɔːdə/
ready (adj) /ˈredi/
researcher (n) /rɪˈsɜːtʃə/
roast / roasted (adj) /rəʊst, ˈrəʊstɪd/
[on] safari (n) /səˈfɑːri/
sauce (n) /sɔːs/
scuba diving (n) / ˈskuːbə ˈdaɪvɪŋ/
snake (n) /sneɪk/
special (n) / ˈspeʃəl/
spider (n) / ˈspaɪdə/
spinach (n) / ˈspɪnɪdʒ/
stairs (n, pl) /steəz/
starter (n) / ˈstɑːtə/
still (adv) /stɪl/
[be] stuck (v) /stʌk/

Unit 14 Perfect places

air (n) /eə/
aloud (adv) /əˈlaʊd/
anyway (adv) / ˈeniweɪ/
bagel (n) / ˈbeɪgəl/
bake (v and n) /beɪk/
bargain (n) / ˈbɑːgɪn/
best (adj) /best/
between (prep) /bɪˈtwiːn/
bird (n) /bɜːd/
breeze (n) /briːz/
calm (adj) /kɑːm/
cloud (n) /klaʊd/
coast (n) /kəʊst/
complete (v) /kəmˈpliːt/
countryside (n) / ˈkʌntrisaɪd/
croissant (n) / ˈkwɑːsɒŋ/
culture (n) / ˈkʌltʃə/
curry (n) / ˈkʌri/
degree (n) /dɪˈgriː/
describe (v) /dɪˈskraɪb/
description (n) /dɪˈskrɪpʃən/
distance (n) / ˈdɪstəns/
docks (n, pl) /dɒks/
dramatic (adj) /drəˈmætɪk/
east (n) /iːst/
field (n) /fiːld/
financial (adj) /frˈnænʃəl/

flower (n) /flaʊə/
fort (n) /fɔːt/
friendly (adj) /frendli/
furniture (n) / ˈfɜːnɪtʃə/
gentle (adj) /dʒentl/
grass (n) /grɑːs/
guess (v) /ges/
hill (n) /hɪl/
huge (adj) /hjuːdʒ/
imagine (v) /ɪˈmædʒɪn/
immigrant (n) / ˈɪmɪgrənt/
instruction (n) /ɪnˈstrʌkʃən/
island (n) / ˈaɪlənd/
jellied eels (n, pl) / ˈdʒelid ˈiːlz/
[the] jungle (n) / ˈdʒʌngəl/
lake (n) /leɪk/
live (adj) /laɪv/
lively (adj) / ˈlaɪvli/
massage (n) / ˈmæsɑːʒ/
memory (n) / ˈmeməri/
mile (n) /maɪl/
mind (n) /maɪnd/
mix (n and v) /mɪks/
the moon (n) /ðə muːn/
move (v) /muːv/
noodles (n, pl) / ˈnuːdlz/
orange (adj) / ˈɒrəndʒ/
organic (adj) /ɔːˈgænɪk/
paradise (n) / ˈpærədaɪs/
peaceful (adj) / ˈpiːsfəl/
piece (n) /piːs/
plant (n) /plɑːnt/
plant pot (n) / ˈplɑːnt pɒt/
pollution (n) /pəˈluːʃən/
poster (n) / ˈpəʊstə/
purple (adj) / ˈpɜːpəl/
reflection (n) /rɪˈflekʃən/
river (n) / ˈrɪvə/
sand (n) /sænd/
scenery (n) / ˈsiːnəri/
second-hand (adj) / ˈsekənd ˈhænd/
the sky (n) /skaɪ/
smell (v) /smel/
snow (n) /snəʊ/
south (n) /saʊθ/
stall (n) /stɔːl/
sunny (adj) / ˈsʌni/
sunrise (n) / ˈsʌnraɪz/
sunset (n) / ˈsʌnset/
temperature (n) / ˈtempərətʃə/
through (prep) /θruː/
tiny (adj) / ˈtaɪni/
typical (adj) / ˈtɪpɪkəl/
view (n) /vjuː/
village (n) / ˈvɪlɪdʒ/

wall (n) /wɔ:l/
west (n) /west/

Unit 15 So how are you feeling today?

ambulance (n) / ˈæmbjʊləns/
aspirin (n) / ˈæsprɪn/
break (v) /breɪk/
compete (v) /kəmˈpi:t/
competition (n) /kɒmpəˈtɪʃən/
cough (n) /kɒf/
cure (n) /kjʊə/
dentist (n) / ˈdentɪst/
depressed (adj) /dɪˈprest/
exam (n) /ɪgˈzæm/
facial (n) / ˈfeɪʃəl/
fail (v) /feɪl/
[be] fed up (adj) / ˈfed ˈʌp/
feeling (n) / ˈfi:lɪŋ/
hangover (n) / ˈhæŋəʊvə/
headache (n) / ˈhedeɪk/
heating (n) / ˈhi:tɪŋ/
homework (n) / ˈhəʊmwɜ:k/
illness (n) / ˈɪlnɪs/
immediately (adv) /ɪˈmi:dɪətli/
include (v) /ɪnˈklu:d/
introductory (adj) /ɪntrəˈdʌktəri/
noise (n) /nɔɪz/
outside (adv) /aʊtˈsaɪd/
sauna (n) / ˈsɔ:nə/
[be off] sick (adj) /sɪk/
similar (adj) / ˈsɪmɪlə/
sports car (n) / ˈspɔ:ts kɑ:/
stomachache (n) / ˈstʌmək-eɪk/
tablet (n) / ˈtæblɪt/
till (prep) /tɪl/
tired (adj) /taɪəd/
toothache (n) / ˈtu:θ-eɪk/
traditional (adj) /trəˈdɪʃənəl/
vitamin C (n) /vɪtəmɪn ˈsi:/

Unit 16 A look into the future

ambition (n) /æmˈbɪʃən/
balloon (n) /bəˈlu:n/
book (v) /bʊk/
borrow (v) / ˈbɒrəʊ/
daydream (n and v) / ˈdeɪdri:m/
dream (n) /dri:m/
flirt (v) /flɜ:t/
gossip (v) / ˈgɒsɪp/
hurt (v) /hɜ:t/
intention (n) /ɪnˈtenʃən/
look for (v) / ˈlʊk fə, fɔ:/
[what's the] matter [with] (n) / ˈmætə/

mechanic (n) /mɪˈkænɪk/
palm tree (n) / ˈpɑ:m tri:/
serious (adj) / ˈsɪərɪəs/
stand (v) /stænd/
[bank] statements (n) /steɪtmənt/
[lose your] temper (n) / ˈtempə/
travel agent's (n) / ˈtrævəl ˈeɪdʒənts/

Recording scripts

Recording 7

MR COSENTINI: Good morning. I'm Mr Cosentini.

RECEPTIONIST: Right. Mr Cosentini. Er, how do you spell that?

C: C–O–S–E–N–T–I–N–I.

R: Ah, right. You're in room three o three. That's on the third floor. The lift is just here on the right, sir.

C: OK. Thank you.

R: Here are your keys and enjoy your stay.

Recording 10

1 **MS HATTON:** Hello. I'm Sarah Hatton.

RECEPTIONIST: Right. Ms Hatton. Er, how do you spell that?

MS H: H–A– double T–O–N.

R: Yes. You're in room five one o on the fifth floor.

2 **MR THOMPSON:** Hello. Er, we're Mr and Mrs Thompson. Richard and Patricia Thompson.

R: Er, how do you spell that?

MRS T: T–H–O–M–P–S–O–N.

R: Thank you. You're in room six o nine on the sixth floor.

3 **MR FITZGERALD:** Good afternoon. My name's Fitzgerald. John Fitzgerald.

R: Sorry, Fitzgerald? How do you spell that?

MR F: F–I–T–Z–G–E–R–A–L–D.

R: Right. You're in room four seven seven on the fourth floor.

Recording 15

1 **A:** Those oranges and these bananas, please.

B: Right, that's one pound sixteen, love.

2 **A:** Oh good!

B: What?

A: I have four thousand, three hundred and ninety dollars in my bank account.

3 **A:** And there are fifty thousand people here today!

4 **A:** What's the population of Australia?

B: I don't know. About twenty million, I think.

Recording 19

1 **RECEPTIONIST:** Good morning. Oasis Leisure Centre. How may I help you?

WOMAN 1: Yes. I'd like to use the pool today. How much is it?

R: Well, it's £3.20 for adults.

W 1: And what time is it open?

R: It's open from 8 a.m. to 9 p.m every day.

W 1: Right. Thank you.

R: You're welcome.

2 **R:** Good afternoon. Oasis Leisure Centre. How may I help you?

W 2: Are there any exercise classes in the morning?

R: Yes. There's a class on Tuesday mornings from 10 a.m. to 11 a.m.

W 2: I see. Thank you. How much is it?

R: Just a moment. It's £7.00 a class.

W 2: I see. Thank you very much.

R: Not at all. You're welcome.

3 **R:** Oasis Leisure Centre. How may I help you?

MAN: Good evening. Are the tennis courts open every day?

R: Yes, sir – every day from 10 a.m. to 9 p.m. except Monday.

M: And how much is it?

R: It's £6.50 an hour.

M: I see. Thank you very much.

R: You're welcome, sir.

Recording 23

NICKIE: Carol's awful.

MAN: Oh, I know. It says "No Smoking" in reception but she often smokes.

N: Yeah. And she always phones her friends from work.

M: Really?

N: Yeah. And she usually takes very long coffee breaks.

M: Oh, she never gives messages!

N: Oh, I know. That makes me really angry!

M: And she sometimes argues with the boss!

N: And she hardly ever smiles!

M: Oh, I hate that! And she's often late in the morning.

N: And another thing! She's always . . .

Recording 29

1 **JANE:** I hate flying. I always get so nervous.

FRIEND 1: Really? I don't mind it.

2 **F 2:** What do you think of the new boss?

J: Oh, I don't mind him. He's OK, but he's very young.

F 2: Oh, I like him. I think he's nice.

3 **F 3:** Do you like football?

J: Yes, I love it. I love watching Walden United play.

F 3: Right . . .

4 **F 4:** What kind of holiday do you like?

J: Oh, I really like lying on a beach and doing nothing. What about you?

F 4: Hmm. I think lying on a beach is a bit boring. I go on a lot of walking holidays.

J: In England?

F 4: Yeah.

J: But it rains all the time.

F 4: Not all the time – and I don't mind the rain.

J: Oh, I like warm weather – sunshine. It always makes me feel good.

5 **F 5:** What do you think of the new café?

J: I don't like it. It's very expensive and the waitresses are very rude.

Recording 30

JANE: Do you want to do this questionnaire?

BOB: Oh, OK. Go on.

J: Right. Do you like talking to friends?

B: Yes, I love it – especially about questionnaires.

J: Do you like going out with friends?

B: Yeah, I do. I like going out with friends.

J: Do you like spending time alone?

B: Mmm. Well, I don't mind it. It's OK.

J: Do you like meeting new people?

B: Well, yes, usually.

J: Do you like going on holiday alone?

B: Oh yes, I really like it. You see . . .

J: Do you like going to parties?

B: I don't mind them – but your party . . .

J: So, do you like staying at home?

B: Um, yeah. I really like staying at home.

J: Right. Do you like doing sports?

B: No, I don't. I like . . .

J: Going for walks?

B: Ugh. No, I hate it. I like . . .

J: What about watching TV?

B: Well, I don't mind it.

J: Do you like active holidays?

B: No, I hate them.

J: Do you like relaxing on holiday?

B: Of course. I love it. Lying on a beach, fantastic . . .

J: Healthy food?

B: No, I don't.

J: Do you like smoking?

B: You know I love it – but I really like . . .

Recording 33

NADIA: Where's Roger tonight?

JANE: Oh, he's at a concert. He's playing with the Brighton Symphony Orchestra!

N: Really?!

J: Oh, yeah. Don't you know? He plays the violin. He can play really well. And he can sing.

N: Really? Well, I know Roger can paint. One of his paintings is in his office. It's beautiful.

J: Is that his painting? I love that painting! Oh, he's so clever – and nice. I really like him.

N: Oh, yeah. He's lovely.

BOB: Oh, Roger! Roger! Roger!

J: Oh, you're just jealous because you can't play the violin, you can't sing and you can't paint.

B: No, I don't like the violin or painting. I'm more interested in sports.

J: Oh, yeah? What sports can you play, Bob?

B: Well, I like swimming.

N: Roger can play tennis really well.

B: Oh, tennis is boring.

J: Do you know? Roger can speak seven languages. What languages can you speak, Bob?

B: Well, I can speak Italian.

J: No, you can't. You can't speak Italian.

B: Yes, I can. Er, ciao Bella, cappuccino, espresso, dolcelatte . . .

Recording 40

A Oh yes, everything's fine, Mrs Jones. Er, the children are sleeping and I'm reading a book.

B Hello, Mr Smith, I'm sorry Mr Harris is interviewing at the moment. Would you like to leave a message?

C Oh, I'm having a great time, Mum. The weather's great. I'm sitting by the pool. The sun's shining.

D Hello, Mr Jones? I'm finishing the report now. I'll see you in the office tomorrow morning.

Recording 44

1 A: You can't go to school like that!
B: What's wrong?
A: You know what's wrong! Go back to your room now and change!

2 A: You look nice. Where are you going?
B: I have a job interview this morning.
A: Oh. Good luck.

3 A: Look at him! He looks awful!
B: He's really very nice.
A: Yeah, but look at those shorts.

4 A: Well, do you like it?
B: Oh, um, yes, well darling, it's great. But, er, you can't wear that to my boss's party!
A: But it's really fashionable!

Recording 47

NEWSREADER: Good evening. This is the ten o'clock news. Tonight's headlines:
A man died in a London fire.
Hollywood actress, Claudia Campbell, married her teenage musician boyfriend.
And why Walden United football fans love their new star.
A fire destroyed a house in Central London early this morning. Five people escaped when they jumped from a window. One man died in the fire. The emergency services arrived after a young woman phoned them from a mobile phone. Luckily the fire didn't destroy the hotel next door. The police arrested a man in South London this morning.

The American actress, Claudia Campbell, married her eighteen-year-old musician boyfriend, Eddie Fernandez, in Las Vegas last night. The couple only invited friends to the wedding. Eddie Fernandez is Miss Campbell's seventh husband. She divorced her last husband, the boxer, Bruno Heidelberger, after he started a relationship with the nightclub dancer, Divine del Rio.

And now to sport. Walden United's 4–1 victory against Roydon Rovers in last night's match surprised everyone. Sixteen-year-old Andy Dixon played his first match for Walden and scored two goals in the first ten minutes. Roydon Rovers superstar, Gian Carlo Carbonara, didn't play. The Italian injured his leg last week.

Recording 50

JOURNALIST: Hello! I'm here at Shoparama, where some shoppers saw Elvis Presley! It's all very exciting! Excuse me! Sir!

MAN: Yes?

J: Did you see Elvis?

M: Um, no, I didn't.

J: Oh, right, well, thank you very much. Um, excuse me! Madam!

WOMAN: Hello.

J: Did you see Elvis?

W: No, I didn't, but my friend Dolly did.

DOLLY: Yes, I did. I saw him next to the ice-cream freezer!

J: Really? What did you do? Did you speak to him?

D: No, I didn't. I went to my car – and I got my camera – but he left before I came back. I didn't see him again!

J: Oh, I see. Well, thank you very much.

D: Sure.

W: You're welcome!

Recording 53

Example: WOMAN: I'm a teacher.
MAN: Oh, really?

1 I come from Australia.
2 I'm a musician.
3 I live in New York.
4 My name's Rebecca Winkenwerder. . . Oh, sorry. Re–be–cca Win–ken–wer–der. But, just call me Becky.
5 I have five brothers and six sisters.
6 No, thanks. I'm a vegetarian . . . Oh, sorry. A ve–ge–ta–ri–an – I don't eat meat.

7 My mother's Japanese and my father's Brazilian.
8 My address is 57 Groveland Street . . . Oh, Grove–land Street.

Recording 54

NICK: So, what's your favourite place?

HANNAH: Oh, well, I think it's, um, my sister's house.

N: Oh, why?

H: Well, I love where it is. It's near a big city, Seattle – but it's in the middle of a forest. So there are big trees everywhere. She's got a really big window in her kitchen – and the kitchen table is, um, right by this window. So when you get up in the morning, you can sit at the table, have some coffee, and look at the trees. It's beautiful. And she has two horses – so we go riding. It's great. I love staying there.

Recording 62

MR GREEN: Good afternoon, Nina.

NINA: Er, sorry I'm late, Mr Green, but I had a terrible journey to work this morning.

MR G: What?! Again?

N: Yes, um, you see, I missed the bus, and then the next bus was, well, the traffic was terrible. I think there was an accident, and um, the train was late.

MR G: And why did you miss the bus?

N: Um. Oh, sorry, but I got up late – and . . .

MAN: Good morning, everybody. I'm sorry I'm late but my car broke down.

Recording 63

POLICE OFFICER: I'd like to ask you some questions, Ms Jones.

MS JONES: Fine. Go ahead.

P: Right, um, first of all, where were you last Wednesday?

MS J: Last Wednesday I was at the university. You see, I'm a part-time student. I study psychology on Wednesdays.

P: OK and where were you on Thursday?

MS J: Oh, um, I was at the office.

P: Fine. And uh, where were you at six o'clock on Friday?

MS J: Six o'clock? Oh, yes. I was in my car. The traffic was terrible.

P: I see. Right. Um, what about at the weekend? Where were you then?

MS J: Well, I was at home with my family.

P: What? All weekend?

MS J: Yes – all weekend. Why?

P: What about yesterday morning?

MS J: Well. I wasn't at work. I was ill.

P: And what about last night?

MS J: Um, I was at a friend's house.

P: I see. Where were you an hour ago?

MS J: I was in a café. Why? Look. I . . .

P: Thank you, Ms Jones. That's all for now.

MS J: But, I don't understand.

Recording 67

1 TONY: Hello, Nicole. Tony here. I have a great part for you – Violet Duvalier.

NICOLE: Oh? What's she like?

T: She's shy and sweet. Perfect for you.

2 T: Liz, honey. I have a great part for you – Chantalle Duvalier.

LIZ: Oh yeah? What's she like?

T: Well, it's a great part for you. She's really interesting – very rude and selfish and . . .

L: Yeah? How much do I get?

3 T: Hi, Johnny.

JOHNNY: Hiya, Tony. How are you?

T: Fine, fine. Listen, Johnny. I have a great part for you – Randolf Duvalier.

J: Oh yeah? What's he like?

T: Well, he's friendly and sporty – perfect for you!

4 GINA: Hello?

T: Gina darling! I have a great part for you!

G: Oh gee, Tony! Who is it?!

T: Loretta Duvalier.

G: Oh! What's she like? Is she exciting?

T: Well, she's lazy and stupid.

G: Oh . . .

5 T: Hi, Jeff. How's everything?

JEFF: Fine. What's up?

T: Well. I've got the perfect part for you, Jeff. Rick Channing, the private detective, in the film *Rick Channing – Private Detective!*

J: Yeah? So, what's he like?

T: He's cool, man, really cool!

J: Hmm, maybe. Send me the script and I'll look at it.

T: Jeff! Jeff? Don't do this to me!

Recording 68

WILL: Did you have a good weekend?

ROSE: Well, yes and no . . .

W: Why? What happened?

R: Well, first the good news. I finally passed my driving test.

W: Congratulations! That's great!

R: Yeah, thanks. I drove the family to the beach on Sunday.

W: That sounds nice.

R: Yeah, but we had some problems.

W: Oh. What sort of problems?

R: Well . . . The traffic was terrible!

W: Oh, no!

R: Oh yeah! It was awful, really awful. It was very, very hot.

W: Oh, I know. It was terrible yesterday.

R: Anyway . . . It took us six hours to get there!

W: You're joking! Six hours?!

R: Yes. Anyway, we finally got there and we found a lovely little beach. It was beautiful, really beautiful.

W: Yeah?

R: And then it started to rain.

W: Oh, no!

R: So we ran back to the car, and . . .

Recording 69

Example: A: I missed the bus this morning and I was late for work again.

B: Oh, no!

1 A: I'm getting married!

B: Congratulations!

2 A: English is so difficult!

B: Oh, I know.

3 A: I lost my wallet yesterday.

B: Oh, no!

4 A: I met the President of the United States at a party last night!

B: You're joking!

5 A: My wife and I are going to the Caribbean at Christmas.

B: That sounds nice.

Recording 71

MARK: So, what are you doing this weekend?

SUSAN: Well, I'm very busy. Tonight I'm having a drink with Dave. Oh, he's so funny. I always have a great time with him. Then on Saturday morning at ten I'm having a driving lesson.

M: Oh! You're learning to drive!

S: Yes. It's my second lesson. I love it. Anyway, then I'm meeting my sister in the afternoon and we're playing tennis. Oh yeah, and on Saturday night Roger and I are going to a dinner party. Then early Sunday morning we're driving to Roger's parents' house. They've got a lovely house by the sea. It's his grandmother's birthday. She's ninety-nine. And anyway, she's having a big family birthday party in the afternoon. Then, in the evening Roger's flying to New York because he's got a meeting there on Monday. And I'm seeing a film with my friend, Janet. You remember Janet. So anyway, um what about you?

M: Oh, I don't know. Maybe . . .

S: Oh, there's my train. Well, have a lovely weekend, bye . . .

Recording 78

1 INTERVIEWER: What do you usually have for lunch?

WOMAN: Well, I usually just have a sandwich and an apple at my desk in the office. I don't have time for a lunch break!

I: What about yesterday?

W: Yesterday! Well, er, it was my birthday. And my boyfriend met me at the office and er, took me to a really nice restaurant for lunch! So, I had champagne! And some lovely fresh fish, salad, vegetables. Oh, and some wonderful chocolate cake.

2 I: What do you usually have for lunch?

MAN 1: Oh, well, there's a nice Italian restaurant near my office, so I usually go there and um, I have pasta, salad, maybe some fish. I try to eat healthy food.

I: And yesterday?

M1: Oh! Er, I was really busy so I just had a hamburger and some chips.

3 I: What do you usually have for lunch?

M2: I always have meat and two vegetables!

I: Oh! Um, and what did you have yesterday?

M2: The same, of course!

Recording 79

MAN & WOMAN: Good evening.

WAITER: Evening, sir. Terrible night, isn't it?

M: Oh, yes. It's awful!

W: What would you like then, sir?

M: Well, I'd like lamb chops, please. And some chips – and salad.

W: Lamb chops?! Oh, no, sir. There aren't any lamb chops.

M: Oh, I see. Um, well then, what about chicken?

W: Chicken? Oh no. There isn't any chicken – not here.

WOMAN: What about soup? Can I have some soup, please?

W: Oh, sorry. There isn't any soup.

M: Right. What about a sandwich? Is that possible?

W: Well, there's some cheese. Would you like a cheese sandwich, sir?

M: OK.

W: Just a minute . . . No, sorry. There isn't any bread.

WOMAN: Well, what do you have?

W: Well, we have some lovely hamburgers.

M: Well, then. Can I have a hamburger, please?

W: Yes, sir. One hamburger. And what would you like, madam?

WOMAN: The same, please. And some chips.

W: Oh, there aren't any chips.

WOMAN: Are there any crisps?

W: Yes, there are some crisps.

WOMAN: Can I have some crisps then?

W: Certainly, madam. Anything to drink?

M: Is there any beer?

W: Yes sir! Of course!

M: I'd like a beer then please.

WOMAN: The same for me, please.

Recording 80

PRESENTER: This country is famous for its big breakfasts. You know, sausages, eggs, bacon, all that. When tourists think of Britain they think of red buses, black taxis and big breakfasts! But do we really eat big breakfasts? We asked people in Edinburgh and London.

INTERVIEWER: Excuse me.

MAN: Yes?

I: I'm from Radio Six. We're interviewing people about what they have for breakfast. Can I ask you some questions?

M: Yes, all right.

I: Well, do you have a big breakfast? You know, a big "British breakfast"?

M: You mean bacon, eggs and all that?

I: Yeah.

M: Well, I love big breakfasts, but I don't have them very often. I don't usually have time in the week – and I don't want a heart attack! But at the weekend I always have bacon, eggs, sausages, toast, everything.

I: What about in the week?

M: Well, cereal, toast, coffee. I'm too busy for anything else.

I: Well, thanks very much!

M: No problem!

I: Excuse me!

WOMAN: Yes?

I: I'm from Radio Six. Could you answer some questions?

W: Um, OK. What about?

I: Breakfast.

W: Breakfast?! Oh, don't ask me! Coffee and a cigarette, dear. That's my breakfast.

I: Oh right. Thanks.

W: It was a pleasure!

Recording 81

1 EDWINA: I'm really hungry. Where's that waiter? We arrived half an hour ago.

CHARLES: Ah, here he is.

WAITER 1: Sorry, sir. Enjoy your meal.

E: What is this?

C: I think it's a fried egg. This tea is awful. It's hot water!

E: And the bread – it's two weeks old!

C: And this orange juice is out of a carton! Ugh! . . .

C: Waiter! Can we have the bill?

W1: Yes, sir . . . Here you are.

C: Look at this bill!

E: That's ridiculous!

2 E: I love this place. It's so beautiful and the food is so good. What are the sausages like?

C: They're delicious. How are the mushrooms?

E: Wonderful.

C: And what about the eggs?

E: The eggs are . . .

C: Oh look, it's twelve o'clock. Er, waiter, can we have the bill, please?

W2: Here you are, sir.

C: Thank you. Seventy-five pounds seventy-five?

E: Oh, well, I love this place. I know it's expensive, but it's always a pleasure.

Recording 83

FRED: Do you mind if we join you?

DEBBIE: Oh, no, no.

TERRY: No, go ahead.

F: I'm Fred, and this is my wife, Wilma.

T: Hi. I'm Terry.

D: And I'm Debbie.

F: Pleased to meet you.

WILMA: Hello.

F: So, are you enjoying Jamaica?

T: Yes.

D: It's lovely.

W: Yes, we love it. We come here every year. Where are you staying?

D: The Grand Hotel. Do you know it?

F & W: Oh, oh.

T: Oh? What?

F: Well, we stayed there three years ago. We didn't like it.

W: Yes, and it's worse now than it was three years ago.

F: I know. Anyway, we're staying at the Plaza. It's nicer than the Grand.

W: Oh, yes.

D: Oh? Why?

F: Well, the rooms are bigger.

W: And more comfortable.

T: Oh, well, our room's OK.

W: Oh, and the food's better. It's lovely!

D: Oh.

F: Hey! There's a lovely beach near our hotel!

D: Oh, our beach is beautiful.

W: Well, yes, but it's more crowded . . .

F: And smaller . . .

W: And I think the beach near the Plaza is cleaner.

D: Oh, really. Shall we go there tomorrow, darling?

T: Well, I wanted to go to the market and buy some souvenirs tomorrow.

F: Ah! Don't go to the market. There's a little shop near the church. The market's more expensive than the shop and the people at the shop are friendlier. Oh, I bought a lovely . . .

Recording 86

1 MAN 1: Hello, darlin'!

M2: Well, hello there.

WOMAN 1: I just don't believe the difference! I'm a new person! I look younger. My skin feels softer. I'm more beautiful. All this from just a little jar of cream! People think my daughter is my sister!

DAUGHTER: Hi, Mum! This is Jasper, my new boyfriend.

JASPER: Hello, Mrs Davis. Nice to meet you!

W1: Vitayouth! Buy it now!

2 WOMAN 2: I have such a busy life. I don't have time to cook. So, when Friday night comes, I turn to Magic Moments. Romantic meals for two! Food from round the world! Italian! Greek! French! They're quicker. They're easier and they're more delicious than my cooking! And you get two free glasses of wine with every meal! Get that holiday feeling again! Magic Moments! Only five pounds ninety-nine – at your supermarket! Cheers!

M3: Cheers!

Recording 87

LINDA: So, what was Australia like?

PHIL: Well, for a start Australia is much bigger than England.

L: Oh, really???

P: Yes, and I think it's more exciting and more interesting.

L: Oh. Why?

P: Well, the people are friendlier. The shop assistants are more polite. And of course the weather's better. It's warmer. The centre of Sydney is wonderful. It's much more interesting than the centre of London and it isn't as crowded. There's so much to do! And they have fantastic food from all over the world.

L: Yeah, it sounds great.

P: And the women are more attractive! They're sweeter, more . . .

L: Thank you very much.

Recording 89

1 WOMAN 1: I really hate crowds – crowds in the shops at Christmas, crowds at football matches, crowds at pop concerts. I get really frightened.

W 2: Do you know why?

W 1: Yes, I think so. When I was very small, about four or five years old, my mum took me shopping at Christmas and I lost her. A shop assistant found me and we found my mum in the end, but I was really frightened. I cried and cried.

2 **MAN 1:** I really don't like snakes, in fact I hate them. Little snakes, big snakes, all snakes.

M 2: Do you know why?

M 1: I don't know. I just don't like them.

Recording 94

MAN: You're going to make a picture in your mind. Your perfect view. But first, relax and get comfortable. Stop what you're doing. Sit back in your chair and close your eyes. Now, listen, and follow the instructions.

You're looking through a window, at a beautiful view. Your perfect view. Where are you? In the mountains? The desert? Or maybe by the sea? In a big city? Are you in a house? A hotel? What sounds can you hear? Maybe music, or people. Are they talking? Are the birds singing? Or is it very quiet? Just relax and imagine . . .

Now, what time of day is it? Early in the morning? Or is it a warm sunny afternoon? Or evening? Is the weather warm? Cold? Take your time and think about these things . . .

Now, complete your view. What can you see from your window? A forest? A garden? Houses? Boats? What are they like? What colours are they? Green? Blue? Yellow? Red? Purple? Are there any people? What are they doing?

Now, is your picture clear in your mind? Slowly open your eyes . . .

Recording 96

1 **SUE:** Well, Kinsale sounds lovely. What are the people like?

MATT: Oh, they're really friendly. They always say "hello" when they see you and they smile. Irish people love talking and you can always have a good conversation. The people are a lot of fun, too.

S: What's the food like?

M: Well, there's fantastic fresh fish. The salmon is delicious and I love the ham. It's fantastic. When I go there I eat very well.

S: And the weather? What's the weather like?

M: Well it isn't hot. The temperature's never more than about twenty-four degrees, but there are sunny days, and then there are beautiful blue skies, but it also rains a lot. That's why it's so green. Sometimes when it rains the sky gets really black!

S: When's the best time to go?

M: I usually go in the summer, and I think that's the best time.

2 **M:** So, what about Tioman? What are the people like?

S: They're very nice. They smile a lot and they're very friendly. The people who worked in our hotel were very helpful and polite.

M: So what's the food like?

S: Malaysian food is very interesting. A lot of vegetables – very fresh, of course – rice, fish and noodles. Oh and curry – even for breakfast – but I enjoyed it. I had coffee and croissants for breakfast once on Tioman, but I didn't like it. You eat differently in the tropics.

M: Oh, right. And what's the weather like, then?

S: Well, when we were there it was very hot. The temperature was around thirty degrees. But there was usually a lovely breeze off the sea.

M: When's the best time to go?

S: Any time. I'd love to go there now.

Recording 100

MAN: Where's Charlie?

WOMAN: He's off sick. He had a very bad week last week.

M: What happened?

W: Well, for a start, his girlfriend left him.

M: Oh, you're joking! I thought they were serious.

W: They were!

M: Oh, I can't believe it!

W: Yeah, oh, he was really depressed about it. Then his brother crashed his car.

M: Oh no. You mean his new sports car?

W: Yeah. He was really, really angry. Then, he worked till three in the morning to finish that stupid report for Friday.

M: Oh yeah . . .

W: He was really tired on Friday. He didn't even come to the pub after work.

Recording 102

1 **WOMAN:** Oh, I hate my life at the moment. I hate work. I hate the Underground, the traffic. I really want to get away and relax. What am I going to do? The Seychelles look lovely. Simon has been there and he says it's paradise. Well, now I have the brochure. I'm not going to stay in London this winter. I'm going to go to the travel agent's now. I'm going to book a holiday in the Seychelles.

2 **MAN 1:** I don't want to buy a motorbike. I want to buy a car. My girlfriend hates motorbikes. Her brother, Tony, is going to help me look for a car. He's a mechanic. I really want a sports car – a red one. Where am I going to find the money?

3 **WOMAN 2:** Joe and I are going to buy a new house. I want a bigger house and a garden. The children want a swimming pool and Joe wants a tennis court. Joe doesn't want to live in the city. He loves the country. Joe's company's doing very well. We have the money. I'm going to look at some houses tomorrow. But I'm not going to tell Joe. I want to surprise him.

4 **MAN 2:** I'm so fed up. My job's so boring. The same thing day after day. I can't do this for the rest of my life. I want to do something more exciting. More interesting. I want to meet new people. I want to be a nightclub singer. So what am I going to do? I'm going to start singing lessons next month.

Recording 104

MAN: Now, Sheila, tell me what you can see in the picture.

SHEILA: Well, I can see the sea. There's a woman standing in the sea and she's looking at the mountain. There's a palm tree and there are some white fishing boats on the beach. The beach is sandy. There's a man standing near a boat. Oh and there are some flowers and there's a big garden. I think there's a river and there's a big house by the river.

M: Thank you, Sheila. Um, do you wear glasses?

Irregular verb list and Guide to pronunciation

Verb	Past Simple	Past participle	Verb	Past Simple	Past participle
be	was / were	been	sleep	slept	slept
begin	began	begun	speak	spoke	spoken
bite	bit	bitten	spell	spelt	spelt
break	broke	broken	spend	spent	spent
bring	brought	brought	stand	stood	stood
buy	bought	bought	steal	stole	stolen
catch	caught	caught	swim	swam	swum
choose	chose	chosen	take	took	taken
come	came	come	teach	taught	taught
cost	cost	cost	tell	told	told
cut	cut	cut	think	thought	thought
do	did	done	understand	understood	understood
dream	dreamed / dreamt	dreamed / dreamt	wake	woke	woken
drink	drank	drunk	wear	wore	worn
drive	drove	driven	win	won	won
eat	ate	eaten	write	wrote	written
feel	felt	felt			
fight	fought	fought			
find	found	found			
fly	flew	flown			
forget	forgot	forgotten			
get	got	got			
give	gave	given			
go	went	gone / been			
have	had	had			
hear	heard	heard			
hold	held	held			
hurt	hurt	hurt			
keep	kept	kept			
know	knew	known			
learn	learned / learnt	learned / learnt			
leave	left	left			
lose	lost	lost			
make	made	made			
mean	meant	meant			
meet	met	met			
pay	paid	paid			
put	put	put			
read	read	read			
ride	rode	ridden			
run	ran	run			
say	said	said			
see	saw	seen			
sell	sold	sold			
send	sent	sent			
shoot	shot	shot			
show	showed	shown / showed			
shut	shut	shut			
sing	sang	sung			
sit	sat	sat			

Guide to pronunciation

Vowels

/ə/	again, doctor, favourite, finally, seven			
/æ/	cat, glad			
/ʌ/	mum, run			
/ɑː/	half, arm			
/e/	red, any			
/ɪ/	miss, ill			
/iː/	seat, see			
/ɒ/	boss, on			
/ɔː/	forty, awful			
/ɜː/	bird, early			
/ʊ/	put, good			
/uː/	food, true			
/ɪə/	beer, year			
/ʊə/	cure, tourist			
/eə/	hair, care			
/eɪ/	plane, play			
/ɔɪ/	join, boy			
/aɪ/	wife, eye			
/əʊ/	go, boat			
/aʊ/	out, town			

Consonants

/p/	pop, shop
/b/	bike, job
/f/	five, cough
/v/	video, wave
/t/	time, sit
/d/	dad, read
/θ/	thing, healthy
/ð/	then, weather
/tʃ/	church, question
/dʒ/	jar, agent
/s/	soft, rice
/z/	magazine, noise
/ʃ/	shut, ambition
/ʒ/	television, pleasure
/k/	coast, black
/g/	girl, bag
/m/	make, home
/n/	name, fun
/ŋ/	sing, long
/h/	hot, who
/l/	live, level
/r/	rock, married
/w/	wet, away
/j/	yellow, use

Pearson Education Limited,
Edinburgh Gate
Harlow
Essex CM20 2JE
England
and Associated Companies throughout the World.
www.longman-elt.com

First published 1999
Fourth impression 2000
Set in 11.5/13pt Bulldog

Printed in Spain by Gráficas Estella s.a.

ISBN 0 582 30548 9

Illustrated by: Katherine Baxter (Folio), Matt Buckley, Linda Clark
(Black and White Line), David Hine, Tim Kahane, Jane Mjølsness (Tonal
Values), Ben Rowdon, Kath Walker.
Cover illustration by Tim Kahane.

Acknowledgements

The authors and publishers would like to thank the following teachers
for piloting and/or reporting on the manuscript:
In **Argentina**, Monica R. de Bernhardt (Colegio de la Esperanza) and
Fernando Lasala Quintana (Asociación Argentina de Cultura Inglesa); in
Austria, Dagmar Baker (Volkshochschule, Linz); in **Brazil**, Albina
Escobar (freelance Teacher Trainer), Maria Beatriz Meneguetti
(Cultura Inglesa Maringá), Sergio Gabriel (Cultura Inglesa São Paulo),
Maria Purificación Vazquéz (Cultura Inglesa Moóca, São Paulo) and
Rogerio Sanches (Cultura Inglesa Bauru); in **France** Benedict Dupont
(Cel St Nazaire, Gavy Oceani), Elaine Redford (Metaform Langues,
Clermont Ferrand); in **Germany**, Elisabeth Lanchès (Volkshochschule
Offenburg) and Silvia Stephan (English Language Centre, Offenburg); in
Hungary Judit Fehér (Európai Nyelvek Stúdiója, Budapest), Eleanor
Födö-Vargek (Coventry House Language School, Kecskemét), Andrea
Koczka (Ameropa Nyelviskola, Budapest), Éva Malomsoki (Atalanta
International, Budapest) and Mária Rózsa Piti (Coventry House
Language School, Kecskemét); in **Italy**, Graziela Castellani, Myra Evans
(University of Florence), Laura Ferrario (Università Cattòlica del Sacro
Cuòre, Milan) and Sophie Salaman (University of Siena); in **Malta**, Alan
Marsh (NSTS English Language Institute, Valletta); in **Poland**, Ian
Bowman (International House, Kraków), Berta Chojnowska (English
School of Communication Skills, Kraków), Agnieszka Florek
(Politechnika Śląska, Gliwice), Anna Hilgier (Polska Fundacja
Upowszechniania Nauki, Warsaw), Hanna Kaczmarczyk (Centre for
Foreign Language Teaching, Warsaw University), Sławomir Kajko
(Politechnika Śląska, Gliwice), Zofia Lebiedzka (Politechnika Śląska,
Gliwice) and Izabela Nowak (Lion School, Katowice); in **Spain**, Fernando
Alba Navarro (Escuela Oficial de Idiomas de Valdemoro), Angela Baker
(Merit School, Barcelona), Francisco Bazaga Calderón (Escuela Oficial
de Idiomas Jesús Maestro, Madrid), Michael Carter (CLIC/IH Sevilla),
Lisa Inskipp-Hawkins (Brighton Idiomes, Barcelona), Sophia Khan
(Brighton Idiomes, Barcelona), Román Landajo Porta (Escola Oficial
D'Idiomes D'Hospitalet), Blanca Martínez López (Escuela Oficial de
Idiomas, Las Rozas), Javier Moreno Artés (Escuela Oficial de Idiomas,
Alcalá de Guadaira, Sevilla), Isabel Orgillès (Escola Oficial D'Idiomes
D'Hospitalet), Mark Ormerod (Merit School, Barcelona), Carmen
Pujadas (Escuela Oficial de Idiomas, Las Rozas), Ben Rowdon (ESADE,
Barcelona) and Russell Stannard (CLIC/IH Sevilla); in **Turkey** John
Jones and Seyhan Özmenek (ITBA, Istanbul); in **the UK**, Aldona
Gawlinski, Ann Hardy (Shane English School, London), Carolyn Jones
(Bell School of Languages, London), Helen Kay (Embassy Language and
Training Centre, St Leonards on Sea), Denis Lyons (Communicaid
Group, London), Katy Mann (Southgate College, London), Martin,
Melanie Faulmann and the students at Greenhill College, Louise
Matthews (MANCAT, Manchester), Lynne Rushton (Bell School of
Languages, Saffron Walden), Sue Wharton (Aston University Language
Studies Unit) and David Wilkins (Shane English School, London).

The Wavelength publishing team:

Judith King, (Publishing Manager), Sue Ullstein, (Senior Development
Editor), Sarah Crawford, (Editor), Rose Wells, (Editorial Assistant),
Rob Briggs, (Senior Designer), Liz Scurfield, (Senior Designer),
Hilary Morgan, (Picture Editor), Paul Katumba, (Production Controller).

The publishers would particularly like to thank Ruth Atkinson
(freelance) for all her editorial work on this Coursebook.

Photo Acknowledgements

We are grateful to the following for permission to reproduce copyright
photographs:

Ace Photo Agency for 41 middle top (Mauritius), 47 bottom left (Peter
Adams) and 47 top (T & J Florian); AKG Photo London for 49 bottom
middle, 49 top left and 49 top right; All Sport for 16/17 (1) (Zoom), 18
far bottom (Clive Mason) and 18 far top (Mike Powell); Robert Briggs
for 87; British Telecom for 64 bottom; CFCL/Image Select for 14 (9); J
Allan Cash for 18 middle bottom; Colorific for 43, 49 bottom right and
60/61 (5); Comstock for 81 bottom and 83 right; Empics/Barry Coombs
for 41 middle bottom; Greg Evans International for 14 (3), 16/17 (4), 18
bottom, 47 middle and 85 top left; Ronald Grant Archive for 60/61 (4),
60/61 (8) and 80; Robert Harding Picture Library for 94; Hulton Getty
for 35 top and 35 bottom; Image Bank for 31; ISI/Herbert Ohge/Naim
Audio for 14 (6); ITN for 41 top; Kobal Collection for 60 , 60/61 (2)
and 60/61 (3); Magic Travel Group for 10; Pearson Education/Trevor
Clifford for 69; /Peter Lake for 29, 30, 31, 37, 41 bottom, 63, 64, 66 and
/Bill Osment for 16/17 (6), 18 top, 18 middle top, 19, 20, 21, 23, 45, 47
middle left, 48, 55, 71 top, 71 bottom, 73, 83 left and 89 middle left, 89
middle right and 89 bottom; Pictor International for 14 (8); Popperfoto
for 35 middle; Rex Features for 16/17 (3), 49 bottom left, 49 top middle,
60/61 (6) and 60/61 (7); Shakespeare's Globe/John Tramper for 16/17
(8); The Slide File for 88; Spectrum Colour Library for 14 (7), 82/83 (c),
82/83 (h) and 85 middle left; Still Pictures/Kevin Schafer for 47 bottom
right; The Stock Market for 87 inset; Tony Stone Images for 6/7, 14 (4),
16/17 (7), 79, 81 top left, 81 top right, 85 top right, 85 middle right, 88
inset, 89 top; Telegraph Colour Library for 14 (5), 14 (1), 14 (2), 14 (10),
16/17 (5), 16/17 (2), 49 background, 82/83 (a), 82/83 (b), 82/83 (d),
82/83 (f), 82/83 (e), 82/83 (g), 85 bottom.

The back cover photographs of the authors by Charles Yacoub.

We are grateful to the following for their kind assistance with location
photography and research: Bell Language School, Saffron Walden;
Bryant Homes; Michael Cassidy; Fluke Menswear, Bishop's Stortford;
The Friends' School, Saffron Walden; Harlow Market; Paul Keating;
Alison McGowan; NatWest Group Archives; Railtrack.